Idioms, Phrases and One Word Substitution

For All Competitive Exams

B.B. Sinha

UNICORN BOOKS

Publisher

UNICORN BOOKS

F-2/16, Ansari Road, Daryaganj, New Delhi-110002
☎ 011-23262683, 23250704
• *E-mail:* info@unicornbooks.in
• *Website:* www.unicornbooks.in

ISBN 978-81-7806-341-6
Idioms & Phrases and One Word Substitution

Edition: August 2023

Printed at : Param Offsetters, Okhla, New Delhi-110020

PREFACE

Idioms and Phrases endow aesthetics to the writing style of a person. Also, in almost all types of competitive exams, now a days, students' knowledge of English is essentially tested in conjunction with other subjects. With this view, I have gathered this collection with proper understanding vis-a-vis the readers' ability to comprehend appropriate application of these idioms and phrases in sentences.

I have been collecting them for a long time in the past, largely from newspapers. It is a common knowledge that newspapers contain articles written by eminent journalists who are adept in using appropriate sentences containing idioms and phrases, resulting in the reading of their articles enjoyable. It is, therefore, no sheer coincidence that readers will find several idioms and phrases of this collection appearing in newspapers every now and then.

With a view to facilitating the readers, I have classified them in different categories, such as phrasal verbs, those based on colours and general section of idioms and phrases.

The second part of this book is exceedingly useful through the collection of one word substitution. This immensely helps readers learn how to be brief and yet effective in communication with fewer number of words.

I hope the readers will find this book a useful guide, especially for practising based on the question sets given therein.

—B.B. Sinha
Author

By the same author

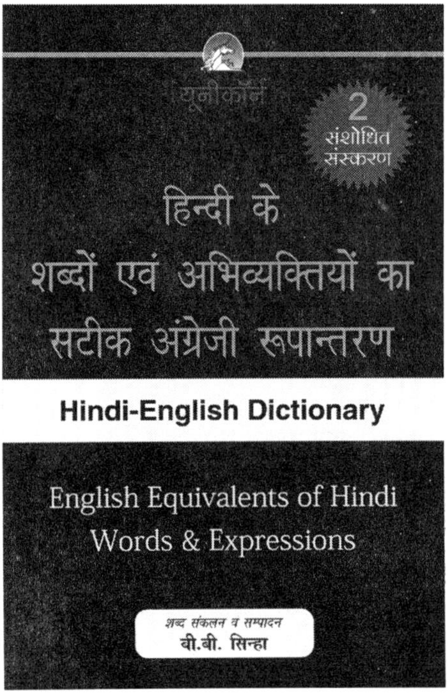

ISBN: 978-81-7806-331-7

U 3317 • ₹400.00

CONTENTS

PART-A

IDIOMS & PHRASES

PART-B

ONE WORD SUBSTITUTION

PART A

IDIOMS & PHRASES

IDIOMS & PHRASES

Definition:

Idiom consists in a set of words for an expression, which bears no direct meaning on the words employed. Thus, idiom carries a peculiar meaning which cannot be construed from the meaning of individual words contained in the idiom. To reiterate, if one attempts to determine the meaning of the idiom by analysing the words constituting the idiom and finding out the individual meaning of the analysed words, the resultant interpretation will be insensible.

For example, 'To talk turkey'.

Phrase is a set of words for an expression whose meaning can be interpreted from the meanings of the individual words composing the phrase.

For example, 'Gird up one's loins'.

PHRASAL VERBS

Back down – concede defeat

Back off – withdraw from action

Back out – withdraw from promise/commitment

Back up – spare copy of necessary data

Blow someone – kill by firing gun away

Blow off – lose temper and give into one's feelings

Blow over – pass off without serious consequences

Blow someone up – explode

Break down – lose emotional control suddenly, sudden functional failure of a machine/equipment.

Break away – escape from control or separate from group

Break in – enter forcibly

Break into – suddenly burst into anger, laughter, singing; to enter by force; to interrupt (a conversation); to begin suddenly (break into a run); to use part of, unwillingly e.g. to break into the money one has saved

Break off – suddenly snap relationship

Break out – sudden happening of fire, hostilities, war, curfew etc.

Break up – item-wise accounting, disperse a crowd

Break with – act in contravention of tradition /customs

Breathe down – to keep too close a watch on what someone is someone's neck doing e.g. Indian students cannot work properly when the Britishers are breathing down their necks all the time

Breathe last – to die

Breathe into – i. to take into the lungs e.g. He became ill after breathing in a lot of coal dust

ii. to listen to closely. She breathed in every word he was saying.

Call back – to summon back; recall; revoke; retract

Call for – demand

Call down – make one appear before someone

Call off – cancel (e.g. demonstration, meeting etc.)

Call in question	–	challenge; throw doubt on
Call to order	–	ask audience to keep silence (e.g. in a meeting)
Call upon	–	go to meet/visit
Call up	–	summon from beneath, or from another world
Carry away	–	take away
Carried away	–	lose self control; to get excited. Martha got so carried away while arguing with her boss as she resigned presently
Carry forward	–	take the figures or data on the next page to continue further; balance in accounting is carried forward
Carry off	–	take away by force
Carry on	–	continue with what one is doing
Carry out	–	perform a task
Carry over	–	keep something to use elsewhere
Carry through	–	bring a task to completion
Check in	–	arrival at a hotel or at airport for stay or travel
Check into	–	enter occupancy in hotel register
Check out	–	enter vacating time in hotel register
Check on	–	verify
Check up	–	investigate; examine
Clear away	–	remove from a place
Clear off	–	go away from a place
Clear up	–	be cured of symptoms
Close up	–	feel blocked, choked
Close on	–	gradually get nearer to (closely on the heels of the enemy)
Close around	–	surround
Close down	–	shut business/shop
Come across	–	meet by chance
Come around	–	recover from shock
Come down (upon)	–	criticize
Come forward	–	come ahead to accept a challenge or responsibility, so as to rise to the occasion
Come about	–	happen, to take place
Come back	–	return; revival; retort
Come before	–	be presented to someone for consideration, discussion and judgement.
Come off	–	succeed; take place; happen.
Come on	–	start doing something

Come out – emerge

Come through – to arrive as expected

i. Have your examination results come through yet? (with) to do what is needed or expected.

ii. I knew that in the end John would come through with the money we needed to survive a risk.

iii. John was so ill as gloomy prognostications were made about him, but despite he (John) survived

Come up – appear unexpectedly as of a problem

Come up against – to encounter a difficulty or confront opposition, e.g. The workers came up against their employer's willingness to pay higher wages despite waranting situations

Cut in – interrupt

Cut off – break connection

Cut out – stop machine's operation; cut out a niche = found a suitable job.

Cut up – behave in unruly manner; cause a person to be emotionally upset.

Cut down – cause to fall by cutting.

Draw back – not to take action because one feels unsure or nervous.

Draw in – come close as of an occasion.

Draw out – become longer in coming of an occasion; hours of day light become longer in spring.

Drop behind – fall back and be left

Drop by or in – visit to meet someone

Drop off – fall

Drop out – cease to take part; e.g. school dropout.

Get across – manage to make idea or proposal known to someone

Get away – escape

Get down to – give serious attention to task/business

Get off – be acquitted of charges/punishment

Get over – recover from a problem; surmount

Get around – manage to deal with a problem

Get through – make contact on telephone

Get up – rise from seat

Give away – hand over prizes etc.

Give in	– surrender, yield to demands
Give out	– stop working due to weariness; emit
Give up	– cease making effort any longer due to losing hope; abandon.
Go about	– carry out a work; pursue.
Go against	– oppose
Go ahead	– proceed
Go along with	– agree to
Go at	– tackle something
Go back on	– fail to keep promise/assurance
Go down	– be defeated in contest; be remembered in history.
Go for	– to assail; to set out to secure; to go to secure or fetch
Go into	– investigate
Go off	– explode as a bomb, gunfire
Go on	– continue
Go out	– be extinguished (of a fire or lights)
Go through	– pass through difficult time/search or examine a document carefully
Go with	– agree to someone
Go without	– suffer lack of something
Hand (something) down	– pass over to successor
Hand (someone) off	– push
Hand (something) out	– disseminate information (press statement); award punishment.
Hand over	– pass to someone else
Hold down	– succeed in keeping; stop a vehicle
Hold off	– fail to occur, resist a challenge or attack
Hold on	– wait, stop
Hold out	– resist difficult situation
Hold for	– continue to demand
Hold over	– postpone something
Hold up	– delay progress
Keep off	– be away from
Keep on	– continue to do
Keep up	– continue progress
Keep up with	– keep oneself aware of
Keep someone up	– keep someone awake

Keep something up	–	continue a course of action
Knock down	–	dismantle
Knock out	–	make unconscious
Lay down	–	formulate rules, conditions
Lay off	–	discharge from work
Lay out	–	spread to full extent
Let down	–	fail to support
Let in	–	allow to come
Let off	–	set free
Let out	–	allow (an opportunity) to escape; to release a person from his unpleasant situation
Let up	–	lessening of intensity; relax one's efforts
Live for	–	regard as the most important in one's life
Live in/at	–	reside
Live off	–	depend on as source of income
Live through	–	survive unpleasant experience
Live in with	–	live with someone without marriage
Look after	–	take care
Look back	–	stop progressing
Look down upon	–	treat with disdain
Look in	–	examine
Look on	–	watch without getting involved
Look out	–	be vigilant for possible danger
Make good	–	to compensate for; to provide restitution or reporation.
Make off	–	to run away; depart hastily.
Make off with	–	to carry away; steal
Make out	–	to write out or complete; to establish/prove (e.g. as a liar); to comprehend; to imply; to suggest (informally meaning for managing or succeeding)
Make over	–	to remodel; alter; to make over a dress/page; to transfer or convey the title deeds of the property
Make up	–	the way anything is arranged, composed or constituted; mental qualities; an actor's materials for personating a part or a woman's cosmetics; to invent
Make up for	–	to compensate for; to make good
Pass by	–	go without notice; hardly aware that it was happening
Pass off	–	happen

Pass out	–	lose consciousness; passing out ceremony for cadets after completing the training
Pass over	–	ignore, avoid
Pick on	–	Single out for unkind remark or treatment
Pick out	–	select from a heap
Pick up	–	gain speed, collect someone from a place
Play about	–	behave in a casual manner
Play down	–	try to lessen the gravity of something happened; belittle.
Play on	–	exploit someone's weak point
Pull back	–	withdraw from doing something
Pull down	–	demolish
Pull off	–	succeed in achieving
Pull out	–	withdraw from a group
Pull through	–	come out of a problem
Put aside	–	keep reserved for future use
Put down	–	suppress rebellion, riot by force
Put off	–	cancel a meeting etc., postpone
Put on	–	become heavier by gaining weight
Put through	–	subject to unpleasant experience
Put up	–	offer a fight or resistance, present a matter for discussion
Put up with	–	tolerate
Run across	–	meet by chance
Run after	–	chase
Run away	–	escape
Run down	–	become weak due to illness
Run into	–	collide
Run off	–	abscond
Run out	–	exhaust
Run over	–	knock down and crush
Set about	–	start doing something; begin a task; informally, attack with blows or words
Set against	–	be in opposition
Set apart	–	keep separate
Set aside	–	keep reserved for some purpose; to rescind an order or cancel or reject a verdict sentence; superseding the judgement of a lower court by an appellate court

Set back	–	delay in progress
Set forth	–	begin a journey; state or describe; present or declare.
Set off	–	explode
Show off	–	display one's ability boastfully; to draw attention by displaying prominently one's accomplishments
Show forth	–	exhibit; expound
Show up	–	expose fault, misdeed etc.; disagree, discredit embarrass or humiliate
Sit in	–	demonstrate in protest
Sit on	–	delay in dealing with something
Sit up	–	be alert
Sit down	–	get ready to start working
Take off	–	be airborne; to embark on a travel
Take (clothes) off	–	remove
Take on	–	accept responsibility etc.
Take over	–	take under control
Take up	–	accept, such as a challenge
Touch down	–	descend on the ground
Touch off	–	ignite or make explode
Touch up	–	make improvement to spruce up
Touch on	–	mention a subject briefly
Touch at	–	stay at a place for brief period
Turn against	–	be hostile
Turn up	–	come to a place
Turn away	–	send back
Turn down	–	reject
Turn off	–	stop machine's operation
Turn on	–	start machine's operation
Turn out to be	–	become known
Turn over	–	hand over control
Turn around	–	change for better
Walk away with	–	steal
Walk away from	–	abandon responsibility
Walk over	–	a race where only one competitor appears, resulting in his easy or unopposed victory
Walk out	–	the act of walking out; to indicate disapproval; a sudden industrial strike.

❑❑❑

IDIOMS BASED ON COLOURS

Black out – sudden temporary loss of consciousness

Be in the black – operate at a profit or be out of debt; have money in one's bank account

Black side – look on the black side of situation i.e. view it pessimistically

Black and white – in written form

Black magic – any of the branches of magic which invokes the aid of demons or spirits as witchcraft or diabolism

Black belt – a symbol of expertise in judo or karate

Black box – flight recorder fitted in aircraft

Black market – market selling illegal and scarcely available items at exhorbitant prices

Black flag – protestors' flag shown to someone as a mark of disrespect

Black list – a list of persons of disrepute who are dis- favoured in dealing with

Black money – ill-gotten money

Black sheep – a member of a group who brings disrepute to the whole group due to his misconduct

Black spot – a spot of disrepute on one's character

Blue baby – a baby whose skin is blue when it is born on account of imperfectly oxygenated blood circulating in its body (cyanosis)

Blue blood – a man of noble family

Blue book – official rules' book

Bule chip – (company or shares) giving high returns/profits

Bule collar – job requiring manual labour

Blue corner notice – police request to international security agencies (interpol) to watch suspect's activities

Blue-eyed boy – person enjoying favours of a powerful man in position

Blue ribbon – which is given to the winner of a competition as a mark of distinction/honour

Green belt – open green land around a city on which building construction is restricted for ecological balance and environmental management

Green card – a document giving a foreigner permission to live and work in the United States

Green fingers (thumb) – a knack of making plants grow well

Greengrocer	–	a shopkeeper selling vegetables and fruits
Green house effect	–	effect of rise in earth's temperature on account of emission of carbon dioxide, methane nitrogen oxide etc. which are considered as ozone depleting substances
Green revolution	–	condition created to increase crop production to feed increasing population
Green room	–	where theatre's actors take rest and prepare themselves for performance on stage with make up
Green signal	–	permission to go ahead
Grey area	–	in a grey area, situation is not clear or where the rules are not known. The difference between gross negligence and recklessness is a legal grey area
Grey eminence	–	eminence grise; a person who exercises power in the background without having authority
Grey matter	–	the ashen grey (the color of the wood ashes) active part of the brain and spinal cord.
Red alert	–	warning to be vigilant
Red card	–	order of referee to a player to leave the ground in a game of football or hockey
Red carpet	–	to accord exceptional welcome
Red corner notice	–	police request to international security agencies (e.g. interpol) to be on the lookout for a wanted criminal
Red cross	–	volunteers' body extending support & relief to victims of war or natural disaster
Red-handed	–	a person caught red-handed means in the very act of crime
Red herring	–	a fact or point in argument which is introduced to draw attention away from the main point.
Red letter day	–	memorable day; specially happy day. It was a red letter day for Paul's family when he came back to the family home.
Red tape	–	excessive adherence to rules causing hurdles
Red signal	–	warning to stop
Red zone	–	dangerous area
White collar job	–	job of sitting in offices
White elephant	–	something which is costly to maintain but not so much worth

White flag – flag shown to enemy to indicate surrender to them

White lie – lie which is harmless

White paper – official document detailing information on a matter of urgent and serious concern.

❑❑❑

PHRASES

Words beginning with — A —

A priori – an opinion is a priori when it is framed on the basis of theoretical knowledge, principles, premises, or deductive reasoning rather than actual experience.

A fortiori – a conclusion, opinion which is having greater conviction, certainty than even the one which formed the basis of the latter conclusion.
* If I cannot do this, a fortiori, neither can you do it.

A la carte – as per the chart or list or menu.
* This hotel serves food items a la carte and charges as per each item.

A la table d'hote – as per fixed rate for a full meal in a hotel.
* Some hotels provide meals a la table d'hote to its customers irrespective of one's diet.

Aces up one's sleeve – a winning plan kept reserved for timely use.

Achilles heels – a vulnerable point in an otherwise redoubtable structure; the great and bold Greek hero in the Trojan war, Achilles was feld by his mother Thetis in his infancy stage on the heel while dipping into the Styx (infernal river) to make him invulnerable.
* Runaway inflation is the Achille's heels in our well thought economic planning.

At odds – at variance

Ad hoc – for the purpose at hand.
* Central government granted ad hoc money for relief work in the food affected areas.
* Ad hoc appointments are made in an office to meet the sudden extra load of work.
* The country should frame some coordinated policy instead of ad hoc measures to combat poverty and unemployment in the country.

Ad interim – temporary measure pending final solution.

* The government announced ad interim pay hike for employees to give partial respite from price rise pending final decision about the exact quantum of enhancement.
* The court ordered ad interim injunction against government orders.

Ad verbatim – word by word
*He narrated ad verbatim the argument between him and his friend

Much ado about nothing – a lot of fuss over some petty matter.
* Most of the persons entrusted with arrangement of function tend to make much ado about nothing, instead of contributing something silently on the occasion.

(Act) against one's better judgement – Act foolishly.

Agent provocateur – a secretly insinuated person into a group to provoke them to commit crime.
*An unscrupulous group acted as agents provocateurs to foment trouble in population already divided on communal lines.
*Pakistan is alleged to employ agents provocateurs to create an atmosphere of insecurity amongst people of a particular community.

Aide memoir – a brief note on salient points of a text which helps one's memory to recollect it when desired.
* The assistant prepared aide memoir of speech.

Alive and kicking – still living in good health and activated.
* He is still alive and kicking at the age of sixty.

All hell broke loose – widespread chaos erupted suddenly.

Alter ego – a second self; counterpart; double.
* He became my alter ego.
* The alter egos of a political boss followed his suit in resigning their posts in the government

Amicus curiae – friend (Ami) of the court, who advises court of helps in its proceedings.
* The court appointed a social worker as its amicus curiae to report on the plight of slumdwellers.

Arm-in-arm – with the arm of one person being passed through the bent arm of the other.
* Protestors walked arm-in-arm on the street.

At hand – very near, about to occur.
* The final exam is at hand

At home with – be comfortable with

A propos – In reference to; to the purpose; appropriately.

At par/Below par/ Above par – equal/below/above in value to something else

At one's wit's end – at the end of intelligence/ingenuity.
* A person confronted with several problems simultaneously, was at his wit's end to solve them satisfactorily.

At the end of one's tether – a rope, chain which is used to fasten a cattle to restrict its movements, is called tether. It is used in sentences, like "Tether cow to graze." "Tether a balloon with string to the doorknob". This phrase indicates that one's resources, or strength, or patience is almost exhausted.
* An indigent person was at the end of his tether.
* A salaried person reaches the end of his tether by the month end.

At the helms of – be in a position of controlling situation

Words beginning with — B

Back and forth – to and fro.
* Move back and forth

back to back – one behind another.
* They were sitting back to back.

(on) Back foot – on defensive position against accusation.

Back against the wall – in desperate situation.
*All round criticism pushed him with his back against the wall.

Back to square one – return to the starting point.

Back in reckoning – recover one's lost position.

Turn one's back on – to ignore someone.

Balmy days – happy days in life.

Bated breath – held up breathing in anxiety, excitement or impatience.
* He waited for his son's returning home with bated breath.

Bay for blood – hanker for revenge.

Hold /Keep someone at bay keep someone or something some distance away.

Beck and call – ready to obey
* He keeps himself at his boss's beck and call.

Bear in mind – to remember

Bear the brunt of – suffer major cousequence of some injurious action.

Bear grudge – harbour enmity or resentment
* He bears grudge against me.

Beat about the bush – to discuss a matter without coming to point.

Bete noire (French) – the person or thing one dislikes most.
* Poor people are bete noire of sophisticated strata of population.

Beyond the pale – outside the bounds of civilized behaviour.
* Conduct beyond the pale attracts criticism.

Bids one's time – wait for opportune time.
* He bides his time to settle score with his adversaries.

Blaze the trail – do something new in such a way as others follow that. Literally, it means marking out trees in a path for others to follow.
* He blazed the trail in a new branch of science.

Blockbuster – (block + buster) Block means a wide space in a city. A city is divided into many blocks of residential areas.

Bust – to knock, to hit, viz. bust in the nose. Therefore, blockbuster means a powerful thing like a bomb which can knock or destroy the whole block of a city. For that matter, a movie, or a speech which is so effective as to attract the whole city or to impress the whole audience, may be called a blockbuster movie, or speech.

* Rajnikant's films mostly turn into blockbuster movies. (Greatly demanding and successful)

* The new economic measures to control black money may prove blockbusters (highly effective).

* His extempore speech was a real blockbuster.

Go berserk – become uncontrolled in a state of frenzy.

Blanket ban – complete prohibition

Draw blank – be unsuccessful in one's attempt

Blow the whistle – to expose wrong doing against someone.
* He blew whistle against wrong doings going on in his office.

Blow by blow – (describe) events as had happened one by one in logical sequence.

Blow hot and cold – vacillate between hot temper and cool one.

Bog down – be trapped in difficulty

Body blow – severe setback

* Suffer a body blow

Bolt from the blue – sudden and unexpected event causing surprise

* Chinese attack on our country was a bolt from the blue

Bone of contention – source of continuous disagreement

Bonne bouche – literally, "Good mouth". It means supremely dainty.

* Each dish was a bonne bouche.

Bon hommie – Bon – good, hommie – man, people, so, geniality.

* Undying bon hommie (warm nature) radiates from him.

* Christmas bon hommie is enjoyed by all.

* The bon hommie of a family reunion is a nostalgic experience.

Bon vivant – (life – viva) So, one who enjoys a good life.

* He is a prodigious worker and a bon vivant.

* Bon vivants revel in sumptuous food

Bon voyage – It means good journey.

* All of us bade him bon voyage and happy, safe return.

Booby prize – award given to the competitor who finishes last i.e., to the lowest score

(to) Boot – besides, over and above, something extra.

* I swapped my pen with that of my friend and paid him Rs. 5 to boot.

This means that I exchanged my pen with a costlier pen of my friend, and paid him Rs. 5 in addition to my pen, so as to compensate the difference in prices of the two pens.

* He is essentially a scholar, and a musician to boot.

* Mr. Birla, a businessman, was a member of parliament to boot.

Bone of contention – a contentious matter; cause for dispute.

Brace oneself up – to prepare for making efforts to achieve something.

* The party in power is bracing itself up for winning next election to continue in powers.

Break the ice – start talking by breaking initial hesitation in relationship with strangers or enemy

Breathe down – keep close watch over someone; to stress the

		someone's neck importance of it
Bring something home	–	to stress the importance of it impress upon
Bring someone to book	–	to punish/to take someone to task for failure or wrong action
Bury hatchet	–	to stop quarrelling and become friendly.
By all means	–	yes, of course; certainly.
By no means	–	not to inquire into private matters impertinently.
Breathe last	–	to die
By and by	–	gradually
By the way	–	incidently
By and large	–	on the whole
By hook or by crook	–	to achieve something through any means.

Words beginning with C

Carpe diem	–	Carpe – fruit, diem – day. So (enjoy) the fruit of today (without having any concern for the next day). * Improvident persons believe in carpe diem –they wallow in their present even if it spells disaster for future.
Carp and cavil	–	to raise objection on trivial issues. * The losing team began to carp & cavil on referee's decision in the match. * Opposition parties carp and cavil even at well intended measures of the government.
Carte blanche	–	also, charta blanche – Blank Cheque. So, it means allow exercise of full discretionary power.
Casus beli	–	beli – belligerence, anything which is used as excuse for conflict or war. * In our country, the religion has been freely and wantonly used as casus beli between people of different ethnic groups. * Even a minor tiff becomes a casus beli between Israel and the Palestinians.
Catch one's breath	–	to stop running or talking so as to recover from breathlessness.
Cause celebre	–	an incident, case or a topic which has attracted wide attention of public. * Shah Bano case on divorced muslim women's maintenance became a cause celebre in our country. * A sensational case of moral depravity of a

cabinet minister is a potential cause celebre.

Caveat emptor – the principle that the seller cannot be held responsible for the quality of his product unless guaranteed in a warranty (Let the buyer beware).

Caviare to the general – be too refined or delicate to be appreciated by ordinary people.

Carve a niche for oneself – earn a respectable position for oneself in one's field of work/study/research.

Call the shot – take initiative in something by revealing one's intentions.

Call a spade a spade – to speak the plain truth without being delicate or sensitive.

Call it a day – stop activity for the day and go to rest.

Call someone to order– to ask someone to stop disobeying the rules of a formal meeting.

Change one's stance – change one's previously taken stand on a matter.

(on) cloud nine – be extremely elated.

Cock a snook at – to give a damn by joining thumb to one's nose top with rest of the palm wide open.

* The kids cocked a snook at the back of the teacher when he was leaving the class.

* A few in the crowd cocked a snook at the policemen when ordered to disperse.

Cool one's heels – to be forced to wait.

Out in the cold – neglected.

Come a cropper – to fall heavily, to fail completely.

Having reached the final, the British have come a cropper against the more experienced German team.

Come home to roost – to take effect upon the person who has said them.

Come of age – to be matured *Our democracy has come of age

Come to blows – start fighting

Come to grips with – have a firm hold on something

Corpus delicti – corpse (careass) – corporeal, body, delicti means crime. In law, the basic element of a crime, as in murder, the death of the murdered person.

* The criminal tried to dispose of the corpus delicti before he escaped.

Corpus vile – worthless (vile) thing which can be risked by experimenting upon.

* Primates are the corpus vile for medical research.

* Education is a corpus vile which is always subjected to new ideas and fancies.

Coup d' etat – coup – blow, stroke. Therefore, it means a blow imparted to an established rule by using force and eventual capture of that institution.

* In many countries, the governments are very frequently overthrown by coup d' etat, and power captured and wielded by military junta.

Coup d' grace – blow of mercy, so, mercy killing, euthanasia. Also, any decisive, final blow.

* Relatives' right to decide giving coup d' grace to a patient afflicted with a terminal disease is a raging controversy.

* His action was coup d' grace for my faith in him.

Cri d' coeur – Coeur – heart, so, cry coming from the core of the heart. Heart-felt protestations, strong and forceful entreaty.

* His cri de coeur for my help moved me.

* His cri de coeur in his attempt to prove his innocence seems to be genuine.

Cross the Rubicon – Rubicon was a small river between Rome and a province of Roman Empire. Julius Caesar was provincial governor who came in conflict with central ruler over maintaining his own band of army, and eventually crossed the river with his army into Rome to overthrow the central ruler. Therefore, a step which sets the events proceed beyond point of no return; which commits one irrevocably to a cause of action; of which one can say that the 'die is cast' is explained by this phrase.

Cry in wilderness – futile exercise in advocating something to others.

* His all attempts to refurbish the image of his organisation ended in a cry in the wilderness.

Cul-de-sac – literally, it means "Bottom of the bag". Therefore, it means passage with no exit forward, i.e., closed at its one end.

* The clues led the investigator finally into a culde-sac.

Curriculum vitae – personal bio-data, autobiography.

* Applicants for a job are required to send brief curriculum vitae along with other information.

*An interesting curriculum vitae was written by the author.

Curry favour – To flatter to gain favour.

* Bureaucrats are ever eager to curry favour with their political boss.

Cut Gordian knot – When you are unable to untie a complicated knot despite a prolonged effort, you are likely to lose patience and snap the thread instead. In this way, you seek a sudden solution to a complicated problem.

* Alexander-the-Great cut (rather than united) the Gordian knot tied by Gordian the ancient king of Phrygia, who tied a knot in conformity with the prophecy that it was to be undone only by the person who was to rule Asia.

* The rampant corruption has become a Gordian knot. * To import technologies in preference to developing indigenous know-how is akin to cutting the Gordian knot.

Words beginning with — D —

Damocle's sword – A danger continuously hanging over one's head like a sword.

* Damocle's sword of glut and the consequent descending prices is vexing the blue chips of industry.

Damp squib – (something) failing to impress

Dance attendance upon –Behave obsequiously, be at one's beck and call.

* An opportunist will dance attendance upon you till you are useful to him.

Dance to someone's tunes – Act at someone's behest

* An uxorious man will dance to his wife's tune and do nothing without her approval.

Dark horse – A virtually unknown person who suddenly comes in prominence.

* A veteran was defeated by a dark horse in the election.

Day in and day out – Everday without fail; continuously.

De facto – By fact, in actuality, for all practical purposes.

		* There exists a de facto state of war between Israel and Palestinians.
De jure	–	By right; according to law * Pt. Nehru was a de jure litterateur to boot.
Deja vu	–	in any of the arts, unoriginal material, old stuff; an illusion of having experienced before something that is really being experienced for the first time; a form of paramresia (psych.) * A film on British Raj, which has been newly produced, is just a deja vu for us.
Dernier cri	–	The last word; the latest fashion.*The 3-piece suit is dernier cri in winter garment * These particular shoes are dernier cri.
Demier resort	–	Final/last resort/stay/refuge * Shimla is the dernier resort in my current itinerary.
Dog in the manger	–	a person who does not let someone use something even if not needed by him.
Down-to-earth	–	(be) realistic in approach or thinking * A down-to-earth person
Down but not out	–	disappointed at failures but not surrendered
(Take a) dig at	–	criticize someone for his failure
Double entendre	–	a word or expression having two meanings – one of which is risque indelicacy or impropriety; off colour. * A risque strong
(In the) doldrums	–	in stagnant situation, in state of inactivity
Double speak	–	speak in two veins making himself ambiguous
Double standard	–	use a rule unfairly for different people
Dressing down	–	give a reprimand * Give a dressing down to him
Dribs and drabs	–	Miserably small amounts spread over a period of time; bit by bit * Tax collected in dribs and drabs by way of income tax is too insufficient to support even the expenses of the income tax department.
Ducks and drakes	–	It is used "to play ducks and drakes". It means pastime of ricocheting flat stones on still surface of water. So, to throw away heedlessly, or squander, is what it means. *Private teaching shops are playing ducks and drakes with the students' career.

Words beginning with — E

Eminence grise – "Grey eminence" also. It means a confidant of the person in power, who exercises power unofficially.

* The eminence grise sons and daughters of ministers don't hesitate even to humiliate senior bureaucrats, but one day each of them proved himself or herself the nemesis for his or her father.

Esprit d' corps – (vigour and spirit in a body) devotion to the organization to which one belongs.

* The esprit d'corps of the entire regiment dropped when its captain was hit by a bullet of the enemy.

*The esprit d' corps, obedience, and acceptance of responsibility are the essence of an employee * A man with esprit d' corps puts his country before his own self.

(Take) exception to – express strong objection because of being offended.

* He took exception to my remarks against him.

(Look) eye-to-eye – (be) in full agreement

* They look eye-to-eye on this matter.

In the eye of storm – be in the centre of controversy

(To) Eat a humble pie – be humiliated

Eat the cake & have it too – try to gain both ways

Words beginning with — F

Fait accompli – A situation of something already done or accomplished, and is no longer worth arguing against its merits or demerits.

* He made emergency purchasing of stationery and got approval fait accompli.

Far cry – A distant goal. * Even after forty years since independence, emancipation of womenfolk in our society is a far cry.

Faux pas – Blunder, embarrassing act against etiquette.

* The whole plan or strategy to counter enemy attack ended in a fiasco due to a minor faux pas.

* His unpleasant remark in the tea party was a faux pas.

Femme fatale – A woman (femme) who seduces men

In fine fettle – in very good condition of health

(Play) first fiddle – To take leading part. * This scientist played first fiddle in the development of nuclear capability of our country.

(Play) second fiddle – To take subordinate position or role to the one who plays the first fiddle.

* He plays second fiddle to his elder brother and faithfully obeys him.

* A junior officer is always expected to play second fiddle to his senior.

* An uxorious husband plays second fiddle to his wife's wishes.

Fire first salvo – start a fight

(Be) Fit as fiddle – To be in extremely good health without any problem whatsoever.

* After recovering from past illness, he is now fit as fiddle.

Fits and starts – Move ahead, then suddenly stop, and again move and so on.

* He completed his education in fits and starts due to financial reasons.

* War against terrorism is going on in fits and starts for quite some time.

Fight shy – avoid something to face, keep away from

Fly-by-night – (business) not reliable and liable to bust overnight

*Foreign Institutional Investors (F.I.I.s) follow the principle of fly-by-night share business.

Fool's paradise – state of illusory happiness

Foot in mouth – making an embarrassing blunder (remark)

For the asking – (get something) with little effort

(Pick up) the gauntlet – To accept a challenge (gauntlet is the glove with loose wrist portion which a wicket-keeper or a fencer uses in the arena. So when a player or, for that matter, any contestant picks up his gauntlet, it is taken as his accepting the challenge of the opponent.)

Throw the gauntlet – To issue challenge to one's opponent (when a contestant throws a gauntlet on the ground in front of his opponent, it is open for him to accept the challenge, or to turn his back and accept defeat).

Run the gauntlet – To get through an array of hostile opponents in the way who are all out to oppose, criticise, harm.

* The government has to run the gauntlet of press criticisms.

Words beginning with ——— G ———

Get hold of – catch

Get one's deserts – (desert dervied from 'to deserve') To receive reward or punishment as one deserves by dint of one's action.

* Judge awarded to each according to his desert.

* Praising someone beyond just desert is but flattery.

* He won appointment on grounds of deserts rather than through family connection.

Get out of hand – be uncontrolled

Gird up one's Ioins – be ready to fight or face what might come upon someone

Get off the ground – start

* The match just got off the ground

Give a damn – reject scornfully

Give and take – mutual compromise on helping each other

Go abegging – (something) be available, but not wanted by people

* Party tickets for election go abegging because of bad prospect of the party winning elections.

Go to dogs – become very bad

* The state of education in government schools has gone to the dogs

Go whole hog – do something with full energy

* He went whole hog to achieve success

Words beginning with ——— H ———

Have no truck with – have no dealings with someone

Happy-go-lucky – cheerful, without caring for the future

Hand to mouth – manage to live on scanty resources available just to meet bare needs

Hands down – easily

* They won the match hands down

(at) hand – be very near to happen

* Exams are at hand

Hands off	–	not involved * Keep oneself hands off the controversy
Hand in hand	–	together * Mob were moving ahead hand-in-hand
(On) hand	–	be available
Hands in glove	–	work secretly in association with someone
Hang fire	–	Delay in execution * The courts' verdicts on the millions of cases are hanging fire for years together. * The young man is hanging fire about his marriage for the last several years.
Hang in the air	–	Be in incomplete situation * He left the task hung in the air.
Hang in balance	–	be uncertain in outcome * The prisoners' fate hung in the balance. * Have one's head in the cloud – have one's thought far away.
On one's heels	–	to flee from a place
Herculean task	–	a task requiring great strength and effort.
High and dry	–	be in a position of without resources
Hit below the belt	–	to criticise or deal a foul blow in an unfair manner *The common people are often hit by the government below the belt on economic issues.
To the hilt	–	to the maximum extent
Hobson's choice	–	Hobson used to give horse to others on hire. But, he used to force a customer to take the first horse in queue and did not allow him to choose one from the lot. The customer was left with no choice other than to "take or leave it". It means "a compelling situation of accepting one of the two equally detestable or injurious alternatives *Monopoly business forces the commodity on customers as Hobson's choice. * Under-employment is Hobson's choice for an unemployed person as he has to either accept it or suffer penury. * A conquered army is left with Hobson's choice of either accepting defeat or face annihilation. * Developing countries are constrained to accept foreign aids with strings as Hobson's choice.
Hoist with one's	–	Caught or injured by what one **own petard** intended as a trick for others.

Hold fast	–	keep tightly secured
Hold good	–	be valid as of a condition, argument
Hold back	–	hesitate to do something
Hold one's ground	–	refuse to budge
Hold water	–	be sound in logic (about a theory, idea etc.)
No holds barred	–	a fight in which any tactic, howsoever unfair, is used.
On the horns of a dilemma	–	Faced with a choice between things that are equally undesirable.

Words beginning with — I —

Ill at ease	–	feel uncomfortable
Inter alia	–	Among other things * Progress of our country depends upon, inter alia, the industrial growth and generation of employment opportunities. * Success of a project depends, inter alia, upon the quantity and quality of the persons who will execute it.
Inter se	–	Amongst themselves * They resolved the differences inter se. * All the species breed inter se.
In the offing	–	(offing – the part of off-shore sea which is visible from the shore, and is, therefore, not far. So, this phrase means something not far off and is likely to reach or apear in a short while. * A change in the cabinet of ministers is in the offing.
In toto	–	In full, in totality * He accepted my proposal in toto.
In the pink of health	–	in good health
In shambles	–	in chaotic condition
Ins and outs	–	all the details of something
Ipso facto	–	(literally, by the very fact itself.) It means 'by the nature of the act or fact itself'. * Cheating in examination ipso facto is a crime. * Indecent behaviour ipso facto deserves deprecation.

Words beginning with — J —

Jack of all trades	–	a person who does or tries to do many things

		without expertise in any trade
Joust with	–	to cross swords with

***Words beginning with* —— K ——**

Keep someone posted with	–	keep informed of the latest situation
Keep someone at arm's length	–	keep a distance and not make intimacy with someone
Keep abreast of	–	be in up-to-date knowledge of something
Kick up a row	–	start an acrimonious quarrel
Kick someone upstairs	–	remove from powerful post by giving promotion to higher but powerless position

***Words beginning with* —— L ——**

(For a) lark	–	(to do something) for amusement
Laissez faire	–	Let (people) do (as they choose). * Business community has long been demanding laissez faire in industries. * Mob indulged in laissez faire vandalism. * Laissez faire religious practice is the antithesis of fundamentalism.
Leaps and bounds	–	Rapidly *Economy is growing leaps and bounds
Leave in the cold	–	desert someone
Leave in the lurch	–	To abandon someone who deserves help and assistance. * His friends left him in the lurch when he lost his fortune and needed their help.
Lese majeste	–	Crime against king, i.e., ruler, therefore, it means treason. * In despotic regime, criticism of government is tantamount to lese majeste.
Live on the edge	–	be in a precarious condition
Lock horns with	–	engage in conflict with someone
Look askance at	–	take with suspicion * The opposition parties look askance at every measure of welfare by the government.
Look with jaundiced eyes	–	Treat in a prejudiced manner

***Words beginning with* —— M ——**

Magnum opus	–	magnum – big, great, opus – work. So, great work of an artist.

* The Discovery of India is the magnum opus of Pt. Jawaharlal Nehru.

Make good – become rich and successful

Make do with – manage with limited means

Make or break – do or die

Make no bones of – do not hesitate to tell something unpleasant

Make hay while sun shines – make good use of opportunities; take advantage of favourable conditions

Neck and neck – close to each other in competition

Make up one's mind – to make a firm decision

Modus operandi – Way of action/accomplishment of a task.

* To develop concord initially and then deprive of the belongings is the standard modus operandi of local thugs.

Modus vivendi – Temporary solution to a problem worked out, pending the final and permanent solution.

*Modus vivendi was set up between the belligerent parties pending final and permanent agreement of truce or armistice. * "No war" agreement between India and Pakistan would be a modus vivendi which would give a reprieve from spending huge resources on defence. *He worked out a satisfactory modus vivendi (workable agreement) with his life. *Well-intending relatives and friends made him to strike a modus vivendi with his wife, and save the family from ruin.

Words beginning with — N

Nip in the bud – (Nip – to sever, to snap, to bite, to cut) Nip off flower buds. Nip off a proposal. There is a nip in the winter air (– a biting cold). So, 'nip in the bud' means to snap, check, halt something harmful in the very incipient stage. * The rebellion was nipped in the bud by the troops loyal to the government. * It is always prudent to nip a potential administrative problem, or a social, .or communal problem in the bud.

Nip & tuck – So close running that the lead or advantage shifts from one contestant to the other alternately. So, a very close contest.

* They ran nip and tuck. *It was a nip and tuck tournament for both the teams.

* These two students always compete nip and tuck with each other, and nobody can guess who will beat whom in the end.

Noblesse oblige – One's nobility or high position obliges him to conduct himself in generous, honourable, and responsible manners. Duty of a person occupying high position. *Noblesse oblige prohibits one from freely mixing with common people.

* Noblesse oblige of judges demand their above suspicious image in the eyes of the litigants.

Nom d' plume – Additional name used with one's proper name for special effects

* Urdu poets used to assume a nom de plume viz "Dard", "Rahi", etc.

Non sequitur – An inference wrongly drawn from a valid premise. It does not follow inference from premise. * The veiled suggestion to ignore or wink at the widespread corruption because it is global phenomenon, is non-sequitur. (widespread corruption is true & hence a valid premise, but to ignore it on that account is a wrong inference).

Nouveau riche – Newly acquired wealth, devoid of commen surate education, culture or sophistication. *Inferiority complex of nouveau riche made him desirous of fame and respect through wealth.

* Honest public servants have to suffer a grim tribulation when their children too have to compete with their nouveau riches peers in daily life from buying ice-cream to wearing jeans.

Nuts and bolts – basic detail of something

Words beginning with —— O ——

Obiter dictum – Incidental remark; a statement not essential to the main argument.

Odds and ends – miscellaneous articles

Odd man out – Distinguishable from the lot. * A man of his own ideology, he is odd man out of his colleagues.

Of no avail – without getting benefit

Of late – lately, recently

* Daytime is getting warmer of late

Off hand – (deal) in non-caring manner

Off the cuff – spontaneous, unprepared, informal.

* He gave an off the cuff discourse on the topic of discussion.

Off the hook – spared from charges or punishment

Off the mark – get started

Off and on – intermittently, not continuously

Off the track – away from the right path

(sit) On fence – wait for opportune moment to decide on whom to take side with, or avoid taking sides

On the rampage – engaged in violence and looting

On the rocks – in a difficult situation, fighting for existence

On the anvil – (anvil is the block of iron on which smith works.) Therefore, it means something is in the process of being prepared.*Proper fiscal discipline with avoidance of profligacy in economic policies will ensure that successful economic policy is on the anvil.

On one's mettle – On one's best of ability in the face of a challenge *He was put on his mettle by the new challenges in his task * He is on his mettle in the field of literature.

On one's own accord – voluntarily, on one's own volition

Out of the blue – unexpectedly, without warning

Out of order – not being in working order

Of sorts – of inconsequential quality.

* He is a poet of sorts. * He is a student of sorts.

* He is an M.P. of sorts.

Out of sorts – in bad mood * He is feeling out of sorts.

Out and out – completely

Once in a blue moon – very rarely

* He is seen once in a blue moon

On the tenterhook – be in suspense

Over and above – in addition to what you get

Words beginning with — P —

Palmy days – Happy and prosperous period of one's life

Papier mashe/mache – A figure moulded in glued pulp. Hence, unreal, artificial and easily demolished.

*Papier mache aristocracy. * Apapier mache crisis was tauted to gain support in its favour. * A papier mache hero, trepid from within. * A papier mache magnanimity will give way to selfishness at the very first opportunity. *A papier mache facade of harmony will crumble at the slightest jerk.

Pass muster – To pass inspection or examination, hence, found to be satisfactory.

* These excuses will not pass muster.

* Variety of music of sorts pass muster under the name of experiments in this art.

Pass the buck – To shift responsibility on others. * One tends to pass the buck to others for a blunder one commits, but does not hesitate to arrogate others' achievement to himself.

Per se – As such, in itself, intrinsically. *Envy per se is not always bad, because it may be the primus mobile for one's diligent effort to emulate a success, which has caused him envy. * Mere pronouncement of equality before law of the land per se is not enough; its implementation is what that matters.

Personae dramatis – Participants in an actual event.

* The personae dramatis of this new movie contain great names of film industry. * All the personae dramatis in our freedom struggle were accomplished personalities in their respective discipline.

Persona non grata – It means an unacceptable person. * Government declared two officers of a diplomatic mission as persona non grata.

Pip at the post – To defeat at the last moment near the goal post. *The runner-up in the race pipped the front runner at the post.

* Those who slogged for the whole year were pipped at the post by those who never read but had the gumption common sense and initiative of cheating in examinations.

Play to the gallery – Aim to gain popularity by satisfying the people's whims.

Play footsie with – Indulge in intimacy covertly and sometimes with duplicity.

* Politicians play footsie with criminals.

Play down – to treat a serious matter in light manner.

Play safe – be careful in doing something

Play possum – Pretend asleep or dead. * It is difficult to get response from one who is playing possum.

Play truant – be absent from school or workplace

Pour or vent one's spleen upon – To release violently one's latent spite, malignant feelings of anger upon someone (who is made the target of attack).

* His countrymen poured their spleen at his failure by excommunicating him. *The people vent their spleen at the goverment for its failure to maintain law and order.

Pride of place – the most prominent position

Prima donna – The leading person who leads others. Hence, a persona who cannot work under someone else, or as a team-mate. * We are looking for team-mate, rather than prima donna.

Prima facie – At face value *His arguments seem prima facie valid.

Pro tem or Pro tempore – for temporary period

Put paid to – To destroy, demolish * This failure put paid to his pretension to be a good student.

Put someone through their paces – Test someone's physical mental ability/skill. *The players were put through their paces in adverse condition. *Test pilot put the new planes through their paces.

Pyrrhic victory – A victory won at great cost. *The Second World War proved a pyrrhic victory for the Allied countries – millions of lives and stupendous amount of resources were lost in the war.

Put one's best foot forward – start something confidently and impressively

Words beginning with — Q —

Quacks and midget – Pseudo experts and those of no consequence in a matter which needs trained and expert hands * Due to the non-availability of medical facilities in remote villages, quacks and midgets rule the roost.

* Entry of quacks and midgets in industries

requiring sophisticated technologists and experts is a potential hazard.

Queer the pitch – To make a mess of, to botch up a smooth process. * His pyrotechnical speech queered the pitch for ongoing peace negotiation. * A parochial leader is enough to queer the pitch of communal harmony.

Quid pro quo – Something taken or given in return for something else given or taken. *Exchange of quids for quos. * You cannot expect to get prompt service in certain government offices without a quid pro quo. *Bilateral deal between India and a rich nation like USA would ensure the rich party a large quid for minor quo. *It is a folly to grant an increase in status and salary of an employee without insisting upon commensurate quid pro quo.

(on the) Qui vive – Who are you? A sentry on guard challenges with this sentence. "Qui vive" is the equivalent call of a French guard. Hence, this phrase means "To be alert, or be on the look-out for something dangerous."

* A suspicious person is always on the qui vive for his own safety from any possible deceitful action of others around him. *A cautious worker is always on the qui vive for possible errors.

Words beginning with — R

Raise cains over – To make noise over something * The boss raised cains over the late coming of his staff. * The kids were raising cains.

Rap and rend – To seize by hook or by crook * Expedient politicians rap and rend electoral victory and ministerial berth.

Take the rap – To take punishment * He took the rap for the lapses of his subordinates.

Raison d' etre – Reason for, or justification for, existence. * Work seems to be her raison d' etre.

Raring to go – be excited to start something

Reach nadir – go to the bottom of downfall; time of the greatest depression, despair etc. *With this failure, she reached the madir of her career.

Res Judicata – A point/legal point that has been finally decided by the court, and cannot be re-opened, de novo at least between the same two parties.

Ride roughshod over	–	To trample, put down ruthlessly. *He rode roughshod over opponents. * Biased occupants of gubernatorial assignments ride roughshod over constitutional propriety.
Rigor mortis	–	Rigidity of body after death. * A deadbody undergoes rigor mortis in certain hours after death
Rise to occasion	–	to act according to the exigent need of the time
Rub shoulder with	–	be in company of an important person
Rub someone the wrong way	–	to make someone angry
Rule the roost	–	To have full control * The criminals now rule the roost in Indian polity.
(Give) a run for one's money	–	give a tough fight in competition
Run-of-the-mill	–	Constituting an ordinary fair sample; not selected * The quality of our body politic has, of late, been vitiated by the run-of-the-mill politicians who now rule the roost.
Run to seed	–	To exhaust vitality, cease growing, deteriorate extremely. * Let his mind run to seed. * The old man has run to seed.
Be on the run	–	keep fleeing to avoid to be caught
Run with the hare and hunt with the hound	–	have your cake and eat it; to be in advantage both ways by remaining with both sides in a fight; try to remain friendly with both sides in a dispute.
Run from pillar to post	–	to go from one person to another in an attempt to be heard about problems

Words beginning with — S —

Salad days	–	in young days
Savoir faire	–	(Savoir – learning, knowledge; faire – to do) ability to act in society in elegant fashion or according to the demand of the situation on the spur of the moment. *Lacking in savoir faire, he creates a disharmony with whomsoever he deals. * Savoir faire is the cardinal virtue for a diplomat.
Scylla & charybdis	–	An unfortunate situation in which both the alternatives are equally injurious. * Caught between scylla and charybdis, he was forced to choose between his wife and the child

in a difficult delivery.

* The teacher was at a loss in deciding how to make the students understand the subject; he was obviously caught between the Scylla of abstruseness of the subject, and Charybdis of inaccuracy stemming from over-simplification of the matter.

(be in the) Saddle – be in full control of situation

Sold like hot cake – sold quickly because of being in great demand

Settle account with – take revenge

Send shudders down one's spine – To frighten over the possible danger.

* A narrow escape from road accident sent shudders down the motorist's spine.

Short change – To cheat by giving less than what is due.

* Cashier shortchanged him by ten rupees.

* People are shortchanged by pseudo religious saints

Short shrift – (1) A brief respite from work, a limited lease of life. * The salesman in a big shop hardly gets a short shrift during working hours. * Only a short shrift is allowed to students between the two sittings of examinations. * The doctor pronounced short shrift for a few months only to a cancer patient.

(2) Little consideration, summary dismissal. * The insolent head of the department gives short shrift to every suggestion by his juniors/ subordinates.

* He gave short shrift to the silly suggestions.

* Unfortunately, culture and education in our country get short shrift by the policy makers.

Shot in arm – A boost in one's morale

* Indian sports need shot in the arm.

Sine die – (A meeting or assembly) adjourned for an indefinite period. That means this is adjourned indefinitely but not cancelled.

Sine qua non – Indispensable, condition

* A good stock or repertoir of vocabulary is sine qua non for command on English language.

* Journals are sine qua nons for a researcher.

* Diplomat's savoir faire is a virtue sine qua non.

Slip of tongue – speak a wrong thing unwittingly

Smell rat – suspect foul play

(At) snail's pace – move at slow speed

Sotto voce – In low voice, undertone. * Musicians play the finale sotto voce. * Uninterested in the solemn rites, a group of people indulged solecistically in gossiping sotto voce in the back seats.

Sow wild oats – To commit offences which may be ascribed to youthful exuberance.

* Youngsters are wont to sow their wild oats.

Spick and span – Spotless, immaculate, spruced, unblemished. * A spick and span car is its owner's pride. *She keeps her house spick and span.

Spill the beans – cause embarrassment, or to spoil a plan by indiscreetly divulging the secrecy.

Stand a treat – pay the bills for hotel (food) and entertainment for others. * He stood a treat to his pals.

Stand in good stead – To place in advantageous position, to assist. * His hard labour throughout the year stood him in good stead in examinations.

* The non-aligned policy stood the country in good stead

* Your ancestors cannot stand you in good stead if you do not have the ability of your own.

* Without regular stint with the studies, your talent alone cannot stand you in good stead during the course of your educational career.

Status quo ante – In the same state or condition as it was before effecting any change. *The troops were ordered to go to their status quo ante position as per the armistice agreement.

Stick to one's guns – To be firm in one's stand in the face of stiff opposition.

* The industrial employees stuck to their guns on their main demand.

Stand by someone – give support in need.

Storm in a teacup – make serious of a trivial matter.

Suo moto – On one's own initiative, without external prompting. * The government suo moto took the decision to raise the salary of judges. * A court can suo moto take congnizance of government's order which is ultra vires of its constitutional powers.

Words beginning with — T

Take someone for ride– To beguile him, deceive him by a giving high hopes.

* Promises made on the eve of an election are designed to take the constituents for a ride.

* Utopian vision of 21st century as oracled by our new government of computers and hi-fi technologies has successfully taken the whole population for a ride.

Take in one's stride – To pass over an obstacle without any difficulty. * A fortitudinous person takes all trials and tribulations of life in his usual strides.

Talk turkey – Talk bluntly *The chairman talked turkey to the board members and warned them of the company's bleak future.

Throw tantrum – Display violent emotions. * On being denied what he wanted to purchase, the child threw tantrums in the shop itself.

Thumb rule – A premise based on experience and, hence, never to fail. * It is a thumb rule that a kid should never be burdened heavily with his studies.

Tip of the the iceberg – a part of whole which is visible

Through and through – completely, thoroughly

Throw in the towel – to accept defeat; admit that one is defeated.

Tit for tat – retaliate in the same manner

Tongue in cheek – casual (remark), not to be taken seriously. * He made a tongue-in-cheek remark on my misdemeanour.

Tower of babel – utter chaos where no one listens to others

Treasure trove – (A find, discovery) which becomes a source of income. *Alfred Nobel's discovery of explosive mixture became his treasure trove and further paved the way for Novel price. * Industrial growth world over turned the oil wells into a treasure trove for the Arabs.

Trials and tribulations– endurance in a suffering.

*Out of this trial and tribulation will be born a new freedom and glory for all mankind – Churchill. * The epic 'Trials and Tribulations in Abject Poverty' is the manifestation of unfaltering faith of our poor mass in their hope for future. * 'The trial and tribulation of South African blacks' is the epic saga of their fight against injustice.

Trigger-happy – ready to open fire from gun at the slightest provocation * A trigger-happy hoodlum is found to suffer punishment under the law.

Triton amongst minnows – One who appears giant among the small ones around it.

* A shark is a triton amongst the minows in the sea.

Trojan horse – During legendary ten-year war between Greeks and City of Troy. Greek soldiers had been hidden inside a huge wooden horse before the rest of the Greek army made a retreat. The wooden horse was dragged by the people of Troy inside the fortified city, and then the hidden Greek army suddenly came out and opened the gate of the fort of the City of Troy. The main bulk of Greek army forced its way into the city, which resulted in the defeat of the City of Troy. Hence, it means a trick, ploy, ruse implanted into the enemy camp to destroy it.

*The international level of financial espionage involves the use of someone as Trojan horse to beat the rivals.

Turn turtle – overturn upside down

Tweedledum and Tweedledee – Two persons or things only nominally different; a nearly identical pair.

* Changing Chief Ministers, rather than policy, is akin to replacing tweedledums with tweedledees.

(It takes) two to tango – nothing is possible to do where at least two are needed.

Words beginning with — U —

Ultra vires – Beyond one's power or authority. * He acted ultra vires in deciding an issue which was not within his powers. *An ultra vires contract.

Up and coming – Enterprising, promising, advancing. *Up and coming entrepreneurs get all the help from the government. * An up and coming organization is expanding its business very rapidly.

Up in arms – To rise unitedly against someone. *The majority of trade unions were up in arms against decreasing the interest on PF deposits.

Upset applecart – spoil a plan

Under duress – (to do something) under threat or pressure

Up to the mark – as per expectations

* His performance is not up to the mark.

Ups and downs – good and bad times in life; vicissitudes

Words beginning with — V —

Volte face – To turn face, turn about of one's opinion/stand. * He made a volte face and turned hostile to his associates.

Vox populi – Vox – voice, populi – people. So, voice of the people or popular opinion.

* Vox populi is the main guiding factor, the government's decisions.

Words beginning with — W —

Wax and wane – Wax – to increase gradually, wane – to decrease gradually. * Waxing and waning of the moon is alternate.

Whipping boy – Someone/something to whom or which onus of every lapse is attributed unjustly.

* Opposition parties are used as whipping boys by the government for disrupted sessions of the parliament.

Willy nilly – Helplessly, inevitably. *Everybody treads willy nilly the trodden path in his social obligations without any effort to improve upon it. *The world is drifting willy nilly towards disaster.

(Take) wind out of one's sails – To outmanoeuvre, to pre-empt one's attempt, to make ineffective.

*The runaway inflation takes wind out of economic planner's sails, and everything goes awry.

*The army's blitz took wind out of the enemy's sails.

Words beginning with — Y —

Yeoman's service – To do some useful and efficient help who is in need.

* Dr. Ambedkar did a Yeoman's service to the nation and the downtrodden people by including several provisions in the constitution to help raise their lot.

❑❑❑

EXERCISES ON IDIOMS & PHRASES

A given phrase (in bold) can be replaced with one of the options mentioned thereunder. Identify which option is the most appropriate.

1. Emancipation of women from social bondage is **a far cry**.
   - (A) Protested widely
   - (B) A matter of crying for women
   - (C) A distant goal to achieve
   - (D) A matter to shout on the offenders
2. Play **ducks and drakes with** serious matters of concern.
   - (A) Treat carelessly
   - (B) Hide one's face from
   - (C) Be concerned with
   - (D) Play game of throwing stones in water
3. Eveyone **plays second fiddle** to the matriarch in the family.
   - (A) Be second in the race
   - (B) Be second in importance
   - (C) Support
   - (D) Have no importance
4. He had a feeling of **deja vu** on his trip to the hill-station after a lapse of two decades.
   - (A) Dejection
   - (B) Nothing new
   - (C) Seeing the same things
   - (D) Great enjoyment of seeing attractive things
5. He was asked by the employer to submit his fresh **curriculum vitae.**
   - (A) Bio-data
   - (B) Games he plays
   - (C) Curriculum of studies
   - (D) Details of what he can do
6. The spectre of ghost **sent shudders down his spine**.
   - (A) Threatened him
   - (B) A chill within his body
   - (C) Jolted his soul
   - (D) Made him unable to stand on his feet
7. My adversary **poured his spleen at** me in his speech.
   - (A) Showered his praise on me
   - (B) Expressed desire to forgive and forget old enmity
   - (C) Vented his accumulated anger against me
   - (D) Spit on me

8. Poor people in this country compromise with fate and work out **a modus vivendi** with the rigours of poverty.
   (A) A way how to live with (B) Surrender before poverty
   (C) A way of living happily (D) A scape from poverty
9. A new law to deal with corruption in public life **is in the offing**.
   (A) Very far in future
   (B) In impossible position to control corruption
   (C) In people's imagination far from reality
   (D) Soon coming
10. The food minister acted as a **dog in the manger** by refusing to distribute rotting grains in open sky.
   (A) Custodian of property as a dog protects his master's house
   (B) A faithful and trusted dog
   (C) A person who neither uses himself nor lets others use
   (D) A miser
11. His all-out efforts to make a plan successful **came a cropper**.
   (A) Proved to be a grand success (B) Failed miserably
   (C) Became a problem for him (D) Cropped up another problem
12. A politician can't ignore a **vox populi**.
   (A) People's problems (B) Threat of becoming unpopular
   (C) Chance to become popular (D) Popular demand of people
13. An emotionally charged person finally **broke down**.
   (A) Became hopeless (B) Became disappointed
   (C) Fell down on the ground (D) Began to weep
14. He **got down** to his task after taking meals.
   (A) Left doing the task
   (B) Gave it to someone else to do
   (C) Started doing or completing his task
   (D) Went to sleep
15. The unending spell of price rise **upset the applecart** of the economy.
   (A) Spoilt the health of the economy
   (B) Overturned people's budget
   (C) Ruined nation's economy
   (D) Disturbed the health of the economy
16. The governments tend to **play down** the challenge posed by the separatists.
   (A) Defeat the challenge

(B) Fight the challenge
(C) Make light of a serious matter
(D) Play hide and seek with the problem

17. **Carry off**.
(A) Continue with work (B) Lose self-control
(C) Perform a task (D) Take away by force

18. **Check in**.
(A) Verify some facts (B) Investigate a crime
(C) Stay in a hotel (D) Fill up a blank cheque

19. **Come down upon**.
(A) Fall on someone (B) Sleep on bed
(C) Criticize someone (D) Throw someone on the ground

20. **Give up**.
(A) Lose hope of (B) Give something to someone
(C) Give awards to someone (D) Give nothing to someone

21. **Turn around**.
(A) Bend something (B) Go in opposite direction
(C) Change in situation for better (D) Change in situation for bad

22. **Black sheep**.
(A) Sheep of black colour
(B) Sheep having black patches on skin
(C) One who brings infamy for his whole social group
(D) Sheep which hides itself in its herd.

23. **White paper**.
(A) Paper of white colour
(B) Paper without anything written on it
(C) Paper on which something is written in invisible ink
(D) Official paper giving information of public matters

24. **Grey eminence**.
(A) On which grey colour is predominant
(B) An eminent person in grey area
(C) An infamous person
(D) A person who exercises power on behalf of another in power

25. **Be at beck and call of someone**.
(A) Be ready to call on someone
(B) Be ready to help someone
(C) Be ready to obey someone
(D) Be ready to be called by someone

26. He is **in fine fettle**.
   (A) in good health
   (B) in fine tune with others
   (C) in good agreement with someone
   (D) ready to play tune on a musical instrument
27. He has **carved a niche** for himself in the society.
   (A) Draw a line
   (B) Earned infamy
   (C) Earned a place of respect
   (D) Dig a hole for keeping valuables
28. He spoke in **double entendre** which was quite in bad taste.
   (A) Double standards
   (B) Ambiguous words
   (C) Using words of two seemingly different meanings
   (D) Double intentions
29. He made a **foot-in-mouth** remark in the meeting.
   (A) Foolish (B) Embarrassing blunder
   (C) Suck foot in one's mouth (D) Wrong
30. Leaders tend to **run with the hare and hunt with the hound** in a matter of social conflict.
   (A) Do two impossible tasks simultaneously.
   (B) Avoid taking sides in a conflict.
   (C) Run behind a hare with hounds.
   (D) Save hare from being killed by a hound.
31. He is a **trigger-happy** person
   (A) Happy to walk with gun
   (B) Happy to kill wild animals
   (C) Happy to fire a weapon
   (D) Apt to open fire at the slightest provocation
32. Their relationship is **on the rocks** due to differences.
   (A) Depends upon rocking performance
   (B) In a bad state with the possibility of breaking down
   (C) In hardship
   (D) As hard to break as a rock.
33. A problem befell him **out of the blue**.
   (A) Unexpectedly (B) While he was living happily
   (C) Once in a while (D) Very rarely

34. The impending court verdict in his case **kept him on tenter hooks**.
    (A) Kept him in constant worries
    (B) Kept him in a state of suspense about what would happen
    (C) Kept him an hooked to it
    (D) Kept him in uncertain situation
35. He asserted that he **had no trucks with** terrorists.
    (A) Did not supply truckload of arms to terrorists.
    (B) Did not drive trucks belonging to terrorists.
    (C) Did not have any relations with terrorists.
    (D) Did not travel together with terrorists.
36. Our team proved **damp squib** in the international matches
    (A) dampened the spirit of opponent teams
    (B) kept their spirit high
    (C) lost hopes of winning
    (D) failed to impress with their performances
37. Mother Teresa will always be remembered for her **yeoman's service** to this country.
    (A) Notable contribution
    (B) Service in yeoman company
    (C) Religious work
    (D) Converting people to Christianity
38. Humiliating electoral defeat **took wind out of the opposition party's sails**.
    (A) Blew up sails off the opposition party's boat
    (B) Thoroughly demoralised the opposition party
    (C) Wind took the opposition party's boat off the course
    (D) Thoroughly destroyed the party's unity
39. The I.I.T.s **have now acquired pride of place** in the world.
    (A) Have become proud of their achievements or popularity
    (B) Have become a matter of pride to get admitted to
    (C) Have become a place to be proud of
    (D) Have earned prominence.
40. Promises made by parties on the election eve are meant **to take voters for a ride**.
    (A) To take voters on a trip to pilgrimmage.
    (B) To promise distribution of cycles to voters in lieu of casting votes

in the party's favour.

(C) To befool voters with false promises which they never intend to fulfil.

(D) To give voters the right to free ride in trains.

41. Regular studies **stand students in good stead** at the time of exams.

(A) Make students stand a good chance to succeed.

(B) Place them in an advantageous position.

(C) Place them in good chance to succeed without studying at the time of examinations.

(D) Stand students to lose at the examinations.

42. Unprecedented success in election gave a **shot in arm** to the party.

(A) Was wounded due to violence in election

(B) Party was wounded due to several leaders leaving the party because of losing prominence in the party

(C) Election was preceded by violence

(D) Party's morale got a boost.

43. The criminal's accomplice **spilled the beans** to the police which was investigating the crimes.

(A) Dilvulged the secrets

(B) Complained against the criminal

(C) Threw the beans in dustbin

(D) Vomitted the beans after eating

44. Babri Masjid demolition **queered the pitch** of communal harmony in the country.

(A) Dug out the pitch to prevent the game

(B) Made a smooth ground for communal harmony

(C) Facilitated communal harmony

(D) Disturbed the atmosphere of communal harmony.

45. A **dark horse pipped the front runner** at the post in a race.

(A) A dark-coloured horse pushed the horse running ahead of it in a race.

(B) A not-so-probable winner went ahead of the frontrunner at the last moment of a race to win the first place

(C) A dark horse won the race easily

(D) A probable winner lost the race to a front runner.

46. Ramcharit Manas is **magnum opus** of Hindu religious epic.

(A) voluminous book

(B) a great work of literature

(C) a great work of creation

(D) the most revered book.

47. Relief materials reach the victims of food in **dribs and drabs**.

(A) Intermittently in small amounts which is insufficient

(B) In sufficient quantity to meet the needs

(C) In excess of what is needed

(D) In the form of unusable materials.

48. He is my bete noire.

(A) Dearest person

(B) Most trusted friend

(C) The most hated person

(D) The best bet

49. We are forced to **willy nilly** take the rising cost of living in our stride.

(A) Wilfully accept calmly as a matter of fact

(B) Unwillingly accept calmly as a matter of fact

(C) Accept, whether you like it or not, as an inevitable fact

(D) Accept without protest and try to overcome this problem.

50. He was ready to help me, but made a **volte face** when time came to help me.

(A) Turned his face in another direction

(B) Suddenly changed his mind

(C) Turned his head upside down

(D) Made a somersault.

ANSWERS

1. (C)	2. (A)	3. (B)	4. (C)	5. (A)	6. (B)
7. (C)	8. (A)	9. (D)	10. (C)	11. (B)	12. (D)
13. (D)	14. (C)	15. (D)	16. (C)	17. (D)	18. (C)
19. (C)	20. (A)	21. (C)	22. (C)	23. (D)	24. (D)
25. (C)	26. (A)	27. (C)	28. (C)	29. (B)	30. (B)
31. (D)	32. (B)	33. (A)	34. (B)	35. (C)	36. (D)
37. (A)	38. (B)	39. (D)	40. (C)	41. (B)	42. (D)
43. (A)	44. (D)	45. (B)	46. (C)	47. (A)	48. (C)
49. (C)	50. (B)				

PART B

ONE WORD SUBSTITUTION

ONE WORD SUBSTITUTION

Words beginning with — A —

Able :

1. Ability to see something which can't be seen normally by others. — **Clairvoyance**
2. Ability to hear a feeble sound which can't be heard by others. — **Clairaudience**
3. Able to be controlled b y someone else. — **Dirigible**
4. Able to be (suitable for) eaten. — **Edible**
5. Able to produce the desired effect. — **Efficacious**
6. Able to achieve accomplishment. — **Effectual**
7. Able to mislead others in conclusion. — **Fallacious**
8. Able to produce offsprings excessively. — **Fecund**
9. Able to produce books excessively or ideas by using creativity, or fruits as by trees. — **Prolific**
10. Able to break down easily. —**Fragile**
11. Able to break due to excess pressure. — **Frangible**
12. Able to be bent around. — **Supple, Lithe, Limber**
13. Able to be bent from straight position. — **Flexible, Pliant**
14. Able to induce laughter. — **Hilarious**
15. Able to cause fire. — **Incendiary**
16. Able to make one forget unpleasant memories. — **Nepenthean**
17. Able to be perceived by sensory organs. — **Palpable**
18. Able to be perceived by ears. — **Audible**
19. Able to be preceived by touch. — **Tactile**
20. Able to feel emotions of pain or pleasure. — **Passible**
21. Able to produce pity. — **Pathetic**
22. Able to be seen through one side to the other. — **Transparent**
23. Able to be seen through one's intention/motive. — **Perspicuous**
24. Able to see through other's intention/motive. — **Perspicacious**
25. Able to be fit for drinking. — **Potable**

26. Able to grasp and hold things. — **Prehensile**
27. Able to sense foreboding about the future. — **Prescient**
28. Able to be persuaded. — **Suasive**
29. Able to suck in. — **Suctorial**
30. Able to induce sleep. — **Sleep-inducing**
31. Able to survive/succeed. — **Viable**

Again :

32. Again lapse into the world of crime after reformed. — **Recidivate**
33. Again happen. — **Recur**
34. Again become worse (condition). — **Exacerbate**
35. Again serve the same food. — **Rehash**
36. Again make a statement (repeat). — **Re-iterate**
37. Again slip into bad condition. — **Relapse**
38. Again and again repetition to memorise a lesson. — **Rote**
39. Again repeat a performance. — **Encore**
40. Again get the sound health after illness (restore health).— **Recuperate**
41. Again take back what was pledged. — **Redeem**
42. Again bring to the good condition. —**Refurbish**
43. Again bring back to the condition of being whole after scattering. — **Redintegrate**
44. Again provide something lost viz. home, limbs. — **Rehabilitate**
45. Again get back which was lost or deprived of. — **Restitution**
46. Again take up the form of a living person, i.e., reborn. — **Re-incarnate**
47. Again come to life after getting destroyed. — **Revive**
48. Again come or send back to one's homeland which one had earlier left for another country. — **Repatriate**

Animal :

49. Animal belonging to the class of cats. — **Feline**
50. Animal belonging to the class of dogs. — **Canine**
51. Animal belonging to the class of cow. — **Bovine**
52. Animal belonging to the class of horse. — **Equine**
53. Animal belonging to the class of goats. — **Capricorn**
54. Animal belonging to the species of sheeps. — **Ovine**

55. Animal belonging to the species of rats. — **Rodent**
56. Animal belonging to the species of snake. — **Reptile**
57. Animal belonging to the species of bear. — **Ursine**
58. Animal living both on land and in water. —**Amphibian**
59. Animal living on land only. — **Terrestrial**
60. Animal living in water only. — **Aquatic**
61. Animal living in sea only. — **Marine**
62. Animal living on trees. — **Arboreal**
63. Animal which feeds on flesh, meat. — **Carnivorous**
64. Animal which feeds on grass. — **Graminivorous**
65. Animal which feeds on shrubs. — **Herbivorous**
66. Animal insect or other invertebrate which feeds on tree branches. — **Phytophagous**
67. Animal devoid of horns. — **Pollard**
68. Animal with one horn only. — **Unicorn**
69. Animal which kills smaller animals to feed on. — **Predator**
70. Animal which is killed by larger animal for food. — **Prey**
71. Animal which feeds on the flesh of its own species. — **Cannibal**

Arranging Styles :

72. Arrangement like that of petals of flower's bud before expansion. — **Aestivation**
73. Arrangement like that of chain. — **Catenation**
74. Arrangement like that of stars. — **Constellation**
75. Arrangement like that of a holy cross. — **Decussation**
76. Arrangement for marshalling the troops/army in such a position as a sweeping fire from along the length of a line of troops/army. — **Enfilade**
77. Arrangement like that of an oriented overgrowth of crystalline material upon the surface of another crystal of different chemical composition but similar structure. — **Epitaxy**
78. Arrangement in a set of (pairs in two each).
79. Arrangement like that of tiles on a slope of thatched roof. — **Imbrication**
80. Arrangement like that of a net. — **Reticulate**
81. Arrangement like that of an inverted pyramid or a spinning top. — **Turbinate**

82. Arrangement like that of spokes in a cycle wheel. — **Verticillate**
83. Artist who makes solid figures by cutting metals or stone.— **Sculptor**
84. Artist who makes portraits on plain sheets. — **Painter**
85. Artist who performs on stage, e.g., dancer or singer. — **Artiste**
86. Artist who entertains villagers by singing folk songs by moving from village to village. — **Minstrel**
87. Artist who produces music by whistling his mouth. — **Siffleur**
88. Artist who displays his physical feats on a rope or pole. — **Acrobat**
89. Artist who displays skill of walking on a horizontal tight rope. — **Funambulist**
90. Artist who teaches learners. — **Maestro**
91. Artist of exceptional ability. — **Virtuoso**
92. Artist who is expert in his field. — **Exponent**
93. Artist who entertains with songs of epic or heroic poems. — **Bard**
94. Artist who performs on swinging ladders from the roofs of tents in circus. — **Trapeze artist**
95. Art of writing in beautiful handwriting. — **Calligraphy**
96. Art of making maps. — **Cartography**
97. Art of making ornamental objects with wires of silver gold or other non-ferrous metals. — **Filigree**
98. Art of making various shapes by folding a piece of paper (especially referrring to the Japanese art of tradition). — **Origami**
99. Artificial limbs-making for fitting in place of amputated limbs in a body. — **Prosthetics**

Misellaneous:

100. Attack someone from a hiding. — **Ambush**
101. Attack public property and damage it. — **Vandalise**
102. Attack public property and set it on fire. — **Arson**
103. Age of person when physical changes start taking place.— **Climacteric**
104. Advertising boards erected in public place. — **Hoardings**
105. Advertising messages written on walls. — **Graffiti**

Words beginning with — B

106. Bad conditioned buildings which are in a partially ruined state. —**Dilapidated**
107. Bad conditioned state due to being old. — **Decrepit State**

108. Bad condition state in which something is shaking. — **Ramshakled**

109. Bad conditioned with loosely shaking joints. — **Rickety**

110. Bad conditioned habitation with thickly populated poor inhabitants in squalid houses. — **Slum**

111. Bag which is carried by sailors for keeping odds and ends, e.g., sewing needles, threads buttons etc., besides toiletries. — **Ditty bag**

112. Bag which is carried by travellers; soldier's bag used for rations, extra clothing etc. — **Haversack**

113. Bag which opens up in two equal halves from the middle. — **Portmanteau**

114. Bag which is hung on one's back with the help of two shoulder straps. — **Rucksack**

115. Bag for carrying by hanging it from shoulders. — **Sachel**

116. Bag of small size for packing small amount of something e.g. coffee. — **Sachet**

117. Bag which is made up of two parts each, slung on either side of animal's back. — **Pannier**

118. Bed which is raised on sides to prevent falling of babies. — **Crib**

119. Bed which is foldable on one side of it which is attached or fixed from the side wall. — **Bunk**

120. Bed which is of low height so as to be pushed under another bed when not in use. — **Truckle bed**

121. Bed which can be moved easely on its wheels attached to legs. — **Trundle bed**

122. Bed which is made of a cloth and its ends hanged with poles. — **Hammock**

123. Bending knees before deity in reverence. — **Genuflect**

124. Bending knees before someone in show of courtesy by women. — **Curtsy**

125. Bending one's head after taking out hat from head in a show of courtesy. — **Vail**

126. Bells which are set to produce attuned sound. — **Chime**

127. Bell made of heavy and flat metal piece and struck with hammer to produce loud sound used in stock exchanges. — **Gong**

128. Bell which is set at the roof-top of church. — **Knell**

129. Body part of head and chest portion. — **Bust**

130. Body part below neck and upward of abdomen. — **Thorax**

131. Body part without head, hands and legs. — **Torso**

132. Body part down the chest portion and upward of waist. — **Midriff**

133. Body part of buttocks and thigh together. — **Haunch**

134. Book written by an author whose identity is not known, doubtful or not recognized; uncanonical. — **Apocrypha**

135. Book of selected writings by various authors usually in the same literary form, of the same period or on the same subject. — **Anthology**

136. Book written by an author on his own life. — **Autobiography**

137. Book which is published after the death of its author. — **Posthumous**

138. Book written by an author on someone's life. — **Biography**

139. Buying a commodity in a market and immediately selling in another market at higher price to earn profit on account of differential happening consequently (e.g. between rupee and foreign exchange markets). — **Arbitrage**

140. Behaviour which is appropriate under a given situation. — **Conduct**

141. Behaviour which is appropriate to the status or class to which one belongs. — **Comportment**

142. Behaviour or conduct which is indicated on one's facial appearance. — **Demeanour**

143. Buildings and open land within the boundary of an educational institution. — **Campus**

144. Buildings and open land within the bundary of an office or business. — **Premises**

145. Broken piece of ceramic or metal. — **Shard**

146. Broken piece of glass with sharp edge. — **Shrapnel**

147. Broken piece of wood. — **Sliver**

148. Born-together babies who look alike. — **Identical twins**

149. Born-together babies who are different in looks. — **Fraternal twins**

150. Born-together babies of dog. — **Puppies**

151. Born-together babies of cats. — **Litters (kittens)**

152. Born-together babies of the birds. — **Brood**

153. Born-together babies from the hatching of the eggs of a bird.— **Clutch**

154. Book of film which becomes great success on commercial scale. — **Blockbuster**

155. Bundle of keys. — **Bunch**

156. Bundle of yarn, cotton. — **Bale**

157. Bundle of grapes hanging from one stem. — **Cluster**

158. Bundle of firewoods. — **Faggot**

159. Bundle of grass, hay, etc. — **Sheaf**

160. Bundle of stitching thread. — **Skein**

161. Bundle of personal belongings which is hung from shoulders of a person. — **Swag**

162. Bundle of currency notes. — **Wad**

163. Burial ground consisting of graves. — **Cemetery**

164. Burial place made underground as in church. — **Catacomb**

***Words beginning with* —— C ——**

165. Capable of producing the desired effects. — **Efficacious**

166. Capable of accomplishing what is desired. — **Effectual**

167. Capable of listening to sound coming from very far which a normal person can't. — **Clairsonant**

168. Capable of seeing something very far. — **Clairvoyant**

169. Capable of misleading others to make erroneous conclusion. — **Fallacious**

170. Capable of producing children excessively. — **Fecund**

171. Capable of producing humour, making one laugh. — **Hilarious**

172. Capable of producing or starting a fire easily. — **Incendiary**

173. Capable of easily bent. — **Flexible**

174. Capable of moving around freely in doing work (human body). — **Supple**

175. Capable of making one forget unpleasant memory of sad events. — **Nepenthean**

176. Capable of affecting someone without making him aware of it. — **Subliminal**

177. Capable of seeing in darkness. — **Scotopiac**

178. Capable of being perceived by touch. — **Tangible, Palpable**

179. Careful about minor details in behaviour, work to be done etc. — **Punctilious**

180. Careful about details of doing something because of fear of committing some mistake. — **Meticulous**

181. Careful about doing something due to the concern of being morally wrong. — **Scrupulous**

182. Carriage on which a deadbody is transported to cremation ground. — **Hearse**

183. Compulsory recruitment of young people in armed forces at the time of war. — **Conscription**

184. Copy someone's voice is to. — **Mimic him**

185. Copy someone's mannerisms, in order to make fun on him. — **Caricature**

186. Copy someone's achievements by trying to make similar achievements. — **Emulate**

187. Charging for eatables itemwise on per plate basis. — **Charge a'la' carte**

188. Charging for eatables at fixed rate for full meal per person. — **Charge a' la' table d'hote**

189. Comparison of one thing with another for indicating similarity. — **Analogy**

190. Comparison of one thing with another for indicating differences. — **Disparity**

191. Clever trick employed to deceive others. — **Artifice**

192. Civilian area where soldiers are temporarily lodged away from their contonment. — **Billet**

193. Cultivation of crops. — **Agriculture**

194. Cultivation of flowers. — **Floriculture**

195. Cultivation of such plants in garden as flowers, fruits, vegetables and ornamental plants. — **Horticulture**

196. Cultivation of trees for wood. — **Silviculture**

197. Cultivation of vegetables for the home or market. — **Olericulture**

198. Cultivation of fruits. — **Pomiculture**

199. Custom of marrying outside one's clan. — **Exogamy**

200. Custom of marrying within one's own clan. — **Endogamy**

201. Custom of marrying and having only one wife. — **Monogamy**

202. Custom of marrying and having more than one wife. — **Polygamy**

203. Custom of woman being the head of the family. — **Matriarchy**

204. Ceremony in which medals and honours are bestowed upon winners. — **Investiture ceremony**

205. Child who acquires abilities of a matured person at an age earlier than usual. — **Precocious child**

206. Child of extraordinary ability or intelligence. — **Prodigy**

207. Child who has begun learning to walk on his feet. — **Toddler**

208. Child who has been kept under the tutelage of someone is his.— **Ward**

209. Child who has been found abandoned by parents. — **Foundling**

210. Cheat someone by assuming identity of another person.— **Impersonate**

211. Carriage upon which a deadbody is kept for taking it to cremation or burial ground. — **Hearse**

212. Celebration in which participants indulge in drinking wine and revelry. — **Bacchanalia**

213. Category of art or literature in classification of various types.— **Genre**

214. Category of animal species in classification of various types.— **Genus**

Words beginning with — D —

215. Daring and dangerous activity is. — **Adventure**

216. Deadbody of a human-being. — **Corpse, Cadaver**

217. Deadbody of an animal. — **Carcass**

218. Deficiency of blood in body is. — **Anaemia**

219. Discarding human body of a dead person by its soul. — **Metempsychosis**

220. Discarding of dead skin and wearing new skin in its place by some living being, e.g., snake. — **Ecdysis or Moulting**

221. Discarding of loaded goods or bundles on ship or aeroplane so as to reduce load to save the ship from sinking. — **Jettison**

222. Disease in which the backbone curves in the backward direction. — **Lordosis**

223. Disease in which the backbone curves forward a hunchbacked condition. — **Kyphosis**

224. Disease of hair-fall causing baldness (skin disease). — **Alopecia**

225. Display of a theme through still/motionless statues and scenery as is presented in Republic Day Parade in Delhi. — **Tableau**

226. Divine impulse or inspiration to do something creative is. — **Afflatus**

227. Deprive someone of his voting rights is to. — **Disenfranchise**

228. Daily traveller between home to workplace is. — **Commuter**

229. Disorder prevalent due to lack of governance is. — **Anarchy**

230. Disease which can spread from one to another is. — **Communicable disease**

231. Disease which can spread by touching infected person. — **Contagious disease**

232. Defect which is present in someone since birth is. — **Congenital defect**

233. Dramatic sudden turn of events which change the course further. — **Coup de theatre**

234. Disease which is prevalent in a specified locality or amongst people of a specified place. — **Endemic disease**

235. Disease which is prevalent in all parts of the world. — **Pandemic disease**

236. Disease which affected large population at the same time.— **Epidemic**

237. Date of equal day and night duration. — **Equinox**

238. Design on an ornament or surface made by engraving or indenting. — **Intaglio**

239. Design on an ornament or surface made by projecting out on the surface. — **Relief**

240. Decline in standards from seriousness to trivial state. — **Bathos**

241. Day on which eating meat is forbidden on religious grounds. — **Maigre day**

242. Drain pipe (a projecting spout) usually grotesquely carved, from a roof-gutter. — **Gargoyle**

243. Dress worn by actors which suits their role. — **Costume**

244. Dress which is worn on ceremonial occasions. — **Regalia**

245. Dress which is worn by persons of a particular profession. — **Robe**

246. Dress which is worn on occasions of mourning the death of someone. — **Weeds**

247. Dress worn on the occasion of marriage by a bride. — **Troussea**

Words beginning with —— E ——

248. Edge of upper end of hollow utensil. — **Brim**

249. Edge of rock's top. — **Brink, Precipice**

250. Edge of a cloth which is turned inward and stitched to prevent unravelling. — **Hem**

251. Edge at the top of two slopes joint, e.g., of a thatched roof. — **Ridge**

252. Edge at the lower end of a sloping roof. — **Eaves**

253. Entering of soul or spirit in a new body. — **Metempsychosis**

254. Excessively high flown exaggerated talking. — **Hyperbole**

255. Excessive accumulation of harmful thing which needs to be removed. — **Plethora**

256. Excessively talented child which is rare in a child of his age. — **Prodigy**

257. Extra text or write-up which is added at the end of a text or book is. — **Addendum**

258. Extra chart or table of data which is added at the end of a book or text is. — **Appendix**

259. Excessive sugar in blood due to sugar disease/diabetes is. — **Hyperglycaemia**

260. Event involving large scale destruction is. — **Apocalypse**

261. Economic independence enjoyed by an organization or society is. — **Autarchy**

262. Eater of meat of one's own species. — **Cannibal**

263. Expression to acknowledge the supernatural power of God to save us, viz., God is great!. — **Alleluia/Hallelujah**

264. Endless period of time. — **Eternity**

265. Evening of the day just before the day of important occasion. — **Eve**

Words beginning with —— F ——

266. Fear of dogs one abnormally suffers from — **Cynophobia**

267. Fear of snakes one abnormally suffers from. — **Ophidiophobia**

268. Fear of taking injection (of parenteral medicines). — **Tripanophobia**

269. Fear of number 13 due to superstitious belief. — **Triskaideka phobia**

270. Feeling pleasure on seeing others in distress. — **Schadenfreude**

271. Feeling pleasure in inflicting pain, insult on others. — **Sadism**

272. Feeling pleasure in getting humiliated, insulted by others (morbid gratifi- cation in suffering pain). — **Masochism**

273. Female singer who leads a group song. — **Prima-donna**

274. Female (usually elderly woman) attendant of young unmarried girl going out of house so as to keep watch on her. — **Chaperone**

275. Feeling fear of looking down from a height such as from a high-rise building. — **Acrophobia**

276. Feeling fear of being in an incommodious or closed room. — **Claustrophobia**

277. Feeling fear of seeing a deadbody. — **Necrophobia**

278. Feeling fear of darkness (morbid fear of the night or darkness). — **Nyctophobia**

279. Feeling about something to happen without any reason to think so. — **Intuition**

280. Feeling about something bad to happen/occur. — **Premonition/Presentiment**

281. Feel like someone else is feeling by keeping oneself in place of sufferer. — **Empathize**

282. Feel sorry for someone suffering. — **Sympathize**

283. Feeling about something happening at a distant place. — **Telepathy**

284. Fellow feeling and display of unity and loyalty shown by members of a professional group. — **Esprit d' corps**

285. Fort which is built on a high ground for defence from enemy's attack is. — **Acropolis**

286. Fighting in a public place and breach public peace is. — **Affray**

287. Fit an old model of machine with latest gadgets so as to make it resemble with latest model old machine. — **Retrofit**

288. Flat board of reasonable height of which the speech maker keeps his book, paper from which he reads while making speech. — **Lectern**

289. Flat board which is raised on a tripod to tack drawing paper on it for artist to sketch or paint portrait on the drawing paper. — **Easel**

290. Flat piece of metal which is used to play strings of musical instruments (strum). — **Plectrum**

291. Fluid secreted by flowers which is collected by bees for making honey. — **Nectar**

292. Foul smelling room due to lack of ventillation/due to dampness. — **Musty room/Fetid/Fusty room**

293. Foul smelling breath of someone's mouth. — **Halitosis**

294. Fleeing from place of residence on large scale due to inhospitable conditions. — **Exodus**

295. Free-thinker. — **Esprit fort**

296. Freeing someone from bondage of servitude. — **Enfranchise**

297. Food or drink having very pleasant taste is. — **Ambrosia**

298. False and defamatory statement made about someone. — **Calumny**

299. False and defamatory rumour spread about someone. — **Canard**

300. Freedom to act as one thinks fit. — **Carte blanche**

301. Final blow given to something which ends the life or process. — **Coup de grace**

302. Fragment of crisp eatables like biscuits, cake etc. — **Crumb**

303. Fragment of broken earthenwares. — **Shard**

304. Fragment of stone. — **Scree**

305. Fragment of broken or demolished building materials. — **Rubble**

306. Fragment of broken structure of something. — **Debris**

307. First show of a picture, film, or theatre. — **Premiere**

308. First-time appearance in a role of acting in a film or drama. — **Debut**

309. First-time or chance of doing something, e.g., making speech etc. — **Maiden chance**

310. Feeling of extreme happiness. — **Euphoria**

311. Feeling of extreme joyful excitement. — **Ecstasy**

312. Fact of having accomplished a work leaving others with no option but to accept it. — **Fait accompli**

Words beginning with — G —

313. Game of guessing what someone from his group is trying to tell him by gesturing without speaking a word. — **Charade**

314. Gathering of people for spiritual sermons, discussions, etc. — **Seance**

315. Gathering of people for performing religious activity of devotees on holy river's bank. — **Congregation**

316. Glass container in which water is filled to keep fish for show is. — **Aquarium**

317. Goddess of justice who punishes evil-doers. — **Nemesis**

318. Group of ships or aircrafts owned by someone is. — **Fleet**

319. Group of warships under navy. — **Armada**

320. Group of people collected at a place. — **Crowd**

321. Group of people indulged in unlawful activity. — **Mob**

322. Group of persons assembled to watch a programme. — **Spectators**

323. Group of young women moving together. — **Bevy**

324. Group of cattle. — **Herd**

325. Group of birds. — **Flock**

326. Group of sheep. — **Hirsel**

327. Group of young birds newly hatched together. — **Brood/clutch**

328. Group of disorderly crowd/mob consisting of lower classes.— **Rabble**

329. Group of geese. — **Gaggle**

330. Group or multitude of fishes moving together in water. — **Shoal**

331. Group of bees. — **Swarm**

332. Group of islands in vicinity to each other. — **Archipelago**

333. Group of people engaged in plotting against a ruler (originally formed by five unpopular ministers of Charles II and now refers to any small party for executing some secret design). — **Cabal**

334. Group of people moving together in a company for security, especially for crossing deserts. — **Caravan**

335. Group of singers who sing in church. — **Choir**

336. Group of hired persons to applaud in a meeting. — **Claque**

337. Group of people with similar knowledge or interest. — **Clique**

338. Group of followers of a person. — **Cohort**

339. Group of stars forming a fixed pattern in the night sky.— **Constellation**

340. Group of mourners who join a funeral procession. — **Cortege**

341. Group of persons who jointly operate a ship, aeroplane etc. — **Crew**

342. Group of attendants of a V.I.P. — **Entourage**

343. Group of officials attached to a V.I.P. — **Retinue**

344. Group of military officers who forcibly overthrow ruler and usurp power. — **Junta**

345. Group of experts who discuss a subject. — **Panel**

346. Group of reveller engaged in revelry. — **Rout**

347. Group of symptoms of a disease. — **Syndrome**

348. Group of three gods. — **Trinity**

349. Group of artists performing together. — **Troupe**

350. Group of three persons who jointly exercise powers. — **Triumvirate**

351. Group of criminals engaged in organized crime on large scale.— **Mafia**

352. Group of three persons jointly holding an office. —**Triumvirate**

353. Group of three persons performing in unison. — **Troika**

354. Group of three god-heads joined together each representing particular function, viz. Brahma, the creator, Vishnu, the preservator, and Mahesh, the destroyer. — **Trinity**

Words beginning with — H —

355. Habit of involuntary grinding of teeth in sleep. — **Bruxism**
356. Habit of walking in sleep. — **Somnambulism**
357. Habit of speaking in sleep. — **Somniloquism**
358. Habit of urinating in sleep. — **Enuresis**
359. Habit of lying (telling lies). —**Mythomania/mendacity**
360. Habit of drinking alcoholic stimulants. — **Dipsomania**
361. Habit of purchasing things without having need of them. (The compulsive urge for buying things). — **Oniomania**
362. Habit of striking together nails in rage or pain. — **Gnashing**
363. Habit of indulging in highfalutin talks. — **Megalomania**
364. Hard and thick skin caused by friction. — **Callus**
365. Habit of involuntary urination on bed during sleep. — **Enuresis**
366. Hairs of animals which are soft, and are used for making wool.— **Fur**
367. Hairs of animals which are hard, erect and are used for making brush. — **Bristles**
368. Habit which is in a person since his birth is. — **Innate habit**
369. Hairs which are mix of black and grey. — **Grizzly hairs**
370. Habit of a person which can't be reformed is. — **Incorrigible**
371. Helper of a golfer who carries golf clubs. — **Caddie**
372. Highest point of, or level of something. — **Apex**
373. Highest point of mountains. — **Summit, Peak**
374. Highest point of a structure. — **Vertex**
375. Highest point of elevation or achievement. — **Pinnacle, Zenith**
376. Hole dug in the ground by animal for dwelling. — **Burrow**

Words beginning with — I —

377. Indefinitely long period of time in the past; an age or one of a series of ages; eternity. — **Aeon**
378. Indefinite future (tomorrow). — **Manana**
379. Items of china wares/materials made of china. — **Crockery**
380. Items of materials used for eating, e.g., spoons, forks, etc. — **Cutlery**

381. Items of materials used for keeping or serving food in, and for cooking in kitchen. — **Utensils**

382. Items of materials used for writing. — **Stationery**

383. Imaginary feeling of existence of something. — **Illusion**

384. Imaginary images created in one's dream while in sleep. — **Phantasmagoria**

385. Impossible to be avoided. — **Unavoidable**

386. Impossible to be tamed. — **Indomitable**

387. Impossible to be stopped by struggling against it *Ineluctable destiny. — **Ineluctable**

388. Impossible to do without something because of being essential. — **Indispensable**

389. Incapable of being placated is. — **Implacable**

390. Incapable of being avoided is. — **Ineluctable**

391. Incapable of being defeated. — **Invincible**

392. Incapable of doing any mistake is. — **Inpeccable**

393. Incapable of failing or being unsuccessful is. — **Infallible**

394. Inferior quality of imitation of a literary work. — **Burlesque**

395. Insensitive to other's feelings. — **Callous**

396. Incarnation of God as ordinary human-being, discarding godly attributes for the good of mankind. — **Kenosis**

Words beginning with K

397. Kill someone for alleged offence without legal process, usually in a mob frenzy. — **Lynch**

398. Killing a terminally ill person to spare him of painful condition out of mercy on him. — **Euthanasia**

399. Killing of one's own father. — **Patricide**

400. Killing of one's own mother. — **Matricide**

401. Killing of one's own son or daughter. — **Filicide**

402. Killing of one's own brother. — **Fratricide**

403. Killing of one's own sister. — **Sororicide**

404. Killing of a very large number of people belonging to a particular ethnic group. — **Genocide**

405. Killing of human-beings. — **Homicide**

406. Killing of one's wife. — **Uxoricide**

407. Killing of a parent or a near relative or a revered person. — **Parricide**

408. Lying dormant/inactive is a state of. — **Dormancy**

409. Lying inactive during hot climate is. — **Aestivation**

410. Lying inactive during winter climate is. — **Hibernation**

411. Love amongst people of a religious faith is. — **Agape**

412. Love between two sexes which is intimate but devoid of erotic feelings (love between soul and soul without sensual desire). — **Platonic love**

413. Language of talking by a specified group of people, viz, hawkers. — **Cant**

414. Language of speech or reply having more than one meaning, and hence the speech or reply is not clearly understood is. — **Ambiguous**

415. Language of speech or reply giving two mutually contradictory ideas is. — **Ambivalent**

416. Loss of someone's appetite. — **Anorexia**

417. Loss of hairs, resulting in baldness caused by a nervous disturbance. — **Alopecia**

418. Loss of memory is. — **Amnesia**

419. Loss of ability to smell. — **Anosmia**

420. Living being which lives both in water as well as on earth is. — **Amphibian**

421. Living being which lives only on earth is. — **Terrestrial**

422. Living being which lives only in water is. — **Aquatic**

423. Living form of human being or animal. — **Incarnation**

424. Listening of sound made by heart, lungs, or other body organs with stethoscope is. — **Auscultation**

425. Look around oneself for anything suspect which may cause harm. — **Circumspect**

426. Look within oneself to realise one's own weaknesses or reasons for failures. — **Introspect**

427. Look back in the past to know what went wrong. — **Retrospect**

428. Look back in the past with fond memory of happy moments in life. — **Nostalgia**

429. Lamentation for the dead person. — **Dirge/Threnody**

430. Lamentation for the dead person by weeping. — **Keen**

431. Large-scale leaving of their homes by people. — **Exodus**

432. Large-scale emigration of people of a country to countries around the world. — **Diaspora**

433. Land beside a sea. — **Coast**

434. Land farther away from coast. — **Hinterland**

435. Land beside a river (river-bank). — **Riparian**

436. Leaving of a dead body by soul to take another living body. — **Metempsychosis**

Words beginning with — M —

437. Manner of speaking, pronouncing a word in peculiar manner, or other peculiar behaviour which makes someone distinctly identified with a community, race, or nativity; an old phrase or custom which has no relevance in the present day. — **Shibboleth**

438. Matter which has nothing to do with moral values is. — **Unmoral (Amoral)**

439. Matter which is against moral values is. — **Immoral**

440. Matter which is not concerned with whether morally right or wrong is. — **Amoral**

441. Medals which are hung from the shoulder of a military uniform. — **Epaulette (Epaulet)**

442. Medicine which is supposed to protect or prevent a disease or infection. — **Prophylactic**

443. Medicine which is taken to get relief from fever. — **Febrifuge/Antipyretic**

444. Medicine which has no physically creative effect, given to a patient for humour or gratification. — **Placebo**

445. Medicine which is supposed to be a cure for all diseases. — **Panacea**

446. Medicine which expels worms from patient's intestine. — **Anthelminthic (Anthelmintic)**

447. Medicine as cough syrup, e.g. codeine. — **Antitussive**

448. Medicine which makes one younger and prolongs life. — **Elixir**

449. Medicine which expels cough from chest/lungs. — **Expectorant**

450. Medicine which is prepared by the physician himself and is not available in other medicine shops (patented medicine). — **Nostrum**

451. Male attendant of elderly woman (dancing partner). — **Gigolo**

452. Main substance of a virtue/quality which determines someone's or something's nature. — **Essence**

453. Main substance of a speech or text. — **Gist**

454. Main substance of accusation against someone. — **Gravamen**

455. Moneylender who charges unreasonably high interest. — **Usurer**

456. Model of full-size human being to display new clothes in shops. — **Mannequin**

457. Model of something in miniature size (wax or clay) for the sculptor to copy. — **Maquette**

458. Moneylender who lends money by keeping valuables as deposits to ensure return of loan with interests. — **Pawnbroker**

459. Most attractive item of something, such as a variety entertainment programme, or a substantial course of meal at dinner (feast); the best item. — **Piece de resistance**

460. Memory of dreadful past which keeps haunting the sufferer. — **Nightmare**

461. Memory loss in which a person fails to recognise familiar things or persons, either partially or totally. — **Agnosia**

462. Memory loss due to ageing. — **Senility**

463. Memory loss due to mental disorder. — **Dementia**

464. Monster who spews fire and has body of a serpent and head of a lion. — **Chimera**

465. (Migrate) Enter a foreign country, with the intention to live there permanently. — **Immigrate**

466. Migrate from one's own country to go and live in another country. — **Emigrate**

Words beginning with — N —

467. Narrow passage passing through rows of buildings, park or garden is. — **Alley**

468. Narrow passage passing through rows of sitting chairs is. — **Aisle**

469. Naked saint who does not wear clothes as a religious practice. — **Gymnosophist**

Words beginning with — O —

470. Object belonging to early time which becomes valuable in present time due to its age is. — **Antique**

471. Object of art made by skilled artists. — **Artefact (Artifact)**

472. Ointment which has softening, relaxing or soothing effect on skin. — **Emolient**

473. Object of irrational reverence; a belief in charms. — **Fetish**

474. Object which is used by witches to cause bad luck to someone. — **Hoodoo**

475. Object which is considered by a clan as their identity; superstitious respect as an outward symbol of an existing intimate unseen relation. — **Totem**

476. Object of value which is preserved as prized possession by successive generations in a family. — **Heirloom**

477. Objects which are having historical values and ought to be preserved by successive generations. — **Heritage**

478. Obsessive compulsive habit of drinking alcohol. — **Dispomania**

479. Obsessive compulsive habit of stealing. — **Kleptomania**

480. Obsessive compulsive habit of lying or exaggerating to an abnormal extent. — **Mythomania**

481. Obsessive compulsive habit of setting something on fire.— **Pyromania**

482. Outer protective layer of a tree. — **Bark**

483. Outer protective layer of banana, orange etc., which is easily removed/stripped off. — **Peel**

484. Outer protective layer of fruits which are thick and not stripped off (such as of watermelon). — **Rind**

485. Official who holds the post at present. — **Incumbent**

486. Official who had held the post before the present one (incumbent). — **Predecessor**

487. Official who holds the post after the present one. — **Successor**

488. Object which is preserved for the memory of a dead person – usually the personal effects of the dead person. — **Memorabilia**

489. Object which is preserved for the memory of past event/days. — **Memento**

490. Object which is preserved for the memory of a place visited where it was brought from. — **Souvenir**

491. Object which is preserved as a memory of person who has given it. — **Remembrance**

492. Object made of clay. — **Terracotta**

493. Object made of clay or metal resembling strange face of human or animal and used as drain outlet projected from roof. — **Gargoyle**

494. Pardon granted by the government to the person convicted for crime against the State is. **— Amnesty**

495. Person who receives and sells stolen goods. **— Fence**

496. Person who lives in caves. **— Troglodyte**

497. Person who is hired to insinuate himself in mob to provoke them to resort to violence. **— Agent provocateur**

498. Person who is holding a post without having official power to exercise/ act. **— Functus officio**

499. Person who is used to enhance someone's virtue by contrasting with that of the very person former is called the latter person's. **— Foil**

500. Person who does duty as a substitute of someone during absence is called. **— Locum tenens**

501. Person who inherits or is entitled to inherit an ancestor's property is called. **— Heir**

502. Person who has become feebleminded due to old age. **— Dotard**

503. Person who does not have faith in a particular religion, especially Christianity/Islam, is called. **—Infidel**

504. Person who is simpleton, free from craftiness in dealing; a naive young woman on the stage. **— Ingenue**

505. Person who has become famous with popular achievements and admired by people. **— Legend**

506. Person who has been abandoned by his society and discarded. **— Outcast**

507. Person who lives away from people, or seclusion from society, in an isolated place. **— Recluse**

508. Person who is always ready to come forward to help people in distress. **— Samaritan**

509. Person who takes pleasure in secretly peeping into private affairs of others; a sexual pervert who derives sexual gratification from watching other's sexual acts or objects; a peeping tom. **— Voyeur**

510. Person who derives pleasure by getting hurt by others. **— Masochist**

511. Person who pretends to possess great wisdom. **— Wiseacre**

512. Person who cracks facetious jokes. **— Wag**

513. Person who is castrated in early age so as to grow into a sexless adult. **— Eunuch**

514. Plant (animal) which possesses the organs of both male and female. — **Hermaphrodite**

515. Person who has the misleading appearance of a female. — **Androgyne**

516. Person who belongs to a place since the earliest time is. — **Aborigine of that place**

517. Person who belongs to a place since his birth is. — **Native**

518. Person who flees to evade arrest is. — **Fugitive**

519. Person who flees from workplace or school without permission to evade work or class is a. — **Truant**

520. Person who argues to defend someone's controversial conduct is his. — **Apologist**

521. Person who has left/renounced his belief in party and harbouring rancour against it. — **Renegade**

522. Person who has renounced his belief in his party, religion, or principle and abandoned it without harbouring rancour against it. — **Apostate**

523. Person who renounces his old association or party for personal gain. — **Turncoat**

524. Person who decides about something or someone on his free will is. — **Arbiter**

525. Person who lives a life of extreme self-discipline by denying himself worldly conforms (as a monk does). — **Ascetic**

526. Person who kills a political leader is. — **Assassin**

527. Person who rules with his own absolute power is. — **Autocrat**

528. Person who carries someone's letter to deliver to another person is. — **Bearer**

529. Person who helps others by giving money is. — **Benefactor**

530. Person who receives money as help from others. — **Beneficiary**

531. Person who is fond of reading books, lover or collector of books, is. — **Bibliophile**

532. Person who habitually talks excessively. — **Blabbermouth**

533. Person who is fond of living in a good lifestyle. — **Bon vivant**

534. Person who behaves in amusingly ridiculous manner. — **Buffoon**

535. Person who pretends to be a qualified doctor. — **Quack**

536. Person who pretends to be learned. — **Charlatan**

537. Person who parades/shows off his knowledge. — **Pedant**

538. Persons who are considered to have knowledge about a specified subject. — **Cognoscenti**

539. Person who has acquired expert knowledge in a matter of art is. — **Connoisseur**

540. Person who has equal share with others in property inherited from ancestor is a. — **Coparcener**

541. Person who habitually doubts a belief or existence of something in absence of proof. — **Sceptic**

542. Person who habitually doubts the intention of everyone behind his action, as being surely motivated by self-gain. — **Cynic**

543. Person who is excessively attentive towards his fashionable, stylish appearance. — **Dandy/Fop**

544. Person who is fond of eating without choice of food. — **Glutton/Gourmand**

545. Person who is fond of eating choice food and possesses knowledge about dishes. — **Gourmet**

546. Person who is young and handsome. — **Adonis**

547. Person who excessively boasts about oneself. — **Braggart**

548. Person who spends lot of time sitting in chair watching television. — **Couch potato**

549. Person who is so pessimistic that he always prophesies about impending disaster. — **Cassandra**

550. Person who parades his superior moralistic behaviour. — **Prig**

551. Person who has different standards of behaviour – what he preaches, he does not practise himself. — **Hypocrite**

552. Person who is physically deformed and mental and suffers from defective due to development due to failure of secretion of thyroid gland. — **Cretin**

553. Person who is the natural successor to the ancestral property. — **Heir**

554. Person (or some event) who/which publicly announces something important to come or happen. — **Herald**

555. Person who holds or practises belief which is contrary to religious orthodoxy. — **Heretic**

556. Person living in solitude like a saint for religious practices.— **Hermit**

557. Person who is rowdy and violent trouble-maker. — **Hooligan, Hoodlum**

558. Person who is kept captive for fulfilment of demands of money or conditions. **— Hostage**

559. Person who joins discussion for resolution of dispute between two contenders. **— Interlocutor**

560. Person who acts in the negotiation between two parties for a deal. **— Intermediary**

561. Person who keeps his thoughts within oneself, and does not talk much. **— Introvert**

562. Person who speaks out his thoughts freely. **— Extrovert**

563. Person who has received an award for something. **— Laureate**

564. Person who is educated in a subject of literature. **— Litterateur**

565. Persons belonging to the class of litterateur. **— Litterati**

566. Persons belonging to the class of glamorous profession like cinema, fashion etc. **— Glitterati**

567. Person who is cunning, crafty, and unscrupulous person. **— Machiavellian**

568. Person (rich patron) who generously spends to support activities of art and literature. **— Maecenas**

569. Person who is wealthy and influential businessman. **— Magnate/Tycoon**

570. Person who is very strict about observance of discipline. **— Martinet**

571. Person who sacrifices his life for a lofty cause. **— Martyr**

572. Person who does massage. **— Masseur**

573. Person who does hair-cut. **— Barber/Coiffeur**

574. Person who is expert in cooking. **— Cook/Cordon bleu**

575. Person who does washing of kitchen utensils. **— Scullion**

576. Person (or living organism) which lives at the expense of other person (or organism). **— Parasite**

577. Person who has lost hope in his future. **— Pessimist**

578. Person who is hopeful for his future. **— Optimist**

579. Person who has lost hope or is dejected. **— Despondent**

580. Person who is capable of attracting people to come behind him to wherever he goes. **— Pied Piper**

581. Person who makes new changes in something existing. **— Innovator**

582. Person who is first to explore something new. **— Pioneer**

583. Person who makes a new path for others to follow. — **Trailblazer**

584. Person who helps to give a new direction to fashion. —**Trend setter**

585. Person who hunts to kill animals unauthorisedly in a protected jungle or sanctuary. — **Poacher**

586. Person who is converted to a new religion after deserting own one. — **Proselyte**

587. Person who gets protection of a superior person is his. — **Protege**

588. Person who is the seniormost member of a prominent family.— **Doyen**

589. Person who is the youngest member of a prominent family. — **Scion**

590. Person who spends recklessly. — **Spendthrift, Prodigal**

591. Person who spends judiciously. — **Thrift**

592. Person who (or organization which) undertakes to meet expenses of an event or a good cause. — **Sponsor**

593. Person who is cruel but equally coward. — **Dastard**

594. Person who makes first appearance in a role. — **Debutant**

595. Person who has cultivated interest in fine arts but in a superficial way and without serious purpose. — **Dilettante**

596. Person who sets up a business or enterprise. — **Entrepreneur**

597. Person who is considered a perfect symbol of highest quality of virtue. — **Paragon**

598. Person who is considered the most popular symbol of a particular field of activity. — **Icon**

599. Person or thing which is considered a symbol of good luck for an event like sports, organization etc. — **Mascot**

600. Person who has committed unpardonably serious crime on account of his wickedness and cruelty, and punished for his crime by forfeiture of lands etc. — **Felon**

601. Person who is engaged or betrothed to be married to a woman is her. — **Fiance**

602. Person who is engaged/betrothed to be married to a man is — **Fiance**

603. Person who betrays his own country. — **Traitor**

604. Person who helps enemy country which is at war with his own country. — **Fifth columnist**

605. Person who is rewarded with the power to rule his country in lieu of his help to the invading enemy to conquer it. — **Quisling**

606. Person who harms or destroys the very person who made him powerful; a person who destroys his own creator. — **Frankenstein**

607. Person who entertains spectators with his fight-to-finish with another person or animal (bull) in an arena. — **Gladiator**

608. Product which belongs to a place because it is produced in that place is. — **Indigenous**

609. Person who is substituted for someone in his role. — **Surrogate**

610. Person who is a habitual flatterer in order to please someone. — **Sycophant**

611. Person who is habitually servile to obey someone in order to please him. — **Toady**

612. Person who is strict in matters of discipline. — **Martinet**

613. Person who is a professional bull-fighter in a game of bull-fight. — **Matador**

614. Person who comes forward to help someone in distress. — **Samaritan**

615. Person who lives in cave. — **Troglodyte**

616. Person who is loyal to one's own country. — **Patriot**

617. Person who does not drink wine. — **Teetotaler**

618. Person who suddenly acquires wealth or prominence and becomes arrogant. — **Upstart**

619. Person without home and job and so wandering from place to place. — **Vagabond/Vagrant**

620. Person who suffers from anxiety of getting ill and always trying to find out symptoms in his body, especially abdomen. — **Hypochondriac**

621. Person who is over-concerned with his health. — **Valetudinarian**

622. Person who aspires to emulate another's success, or attain eminence in some area, often vainly. — **Wannabe actor**

623. Person who just failed to become something he would have been, such as a poet, because of defect of character and circumstances, and suffered frustration. — **Poet manque**

624. Person who is fearless is. — **Intrepid**

625. Person who deliberately intimidates those who are weaker. — **Bully**

626. Person who is capable of finding a source of underground water by tapping ground with a divining rod. — **Dowser**

627. Person who has won laurels, awards in any field for distinct achievements. — **Laureate**

628. Person who has the superiormost status amongst members of a group of equals. — **Primus inter pares**

629. Person who takes note of speech/dictation; a copying secretary. — **Amanuensis**

630. Person who practises his profession in unprofessional manners, e.g., a lawyer, doctor, etc.; an unscrupulous practitioner in any business or profession. — **Shyster**

631. Person who cannot be pleased with entreaties. — **Inexorable person**

632. Person who can't do any wrong. — **Impeccable person**

633. Person who cannot be conquered. — **Invincible person**

634. People of a country or race who have scattered throughout the world to live there. — **Diaspora**

635. Person who accompanies old woman when she goes out of house. — **Gigolo**

636. Person who is habitually dirty in appearance, dressing, etc. —**Sloven**

637. Person who is reserved in speaking and hence talks less. — **Reticent person**

638. Person who does not react to provcations; not easily excited by other's actions/utterances. — **Phlegmatic person**

639. Person who acts against established practices in social or religious matters; against worship of images. — **Iconoclast**

640. Person who remains calm in both pain and pleasure. — **Stoic person**

641. Person who hates women. — **Misogynist**

642. Person who hates mankind. — **Misanthrope**

643. Person who habitually flirts with women. — **Philander**

644. Person who loves mankind and generously helps people in need. — **Philanthrope/Philanthropist**

645. Person who is self-centred or selfish. — **Egoist**

646. Person who has tendency to talk about himself and his abilities. — **Egotist**

647. Person who habitually works with his left hand. — **Sinistral**

648. Person who is strictly vegetarian. — **Vegan**

649. Person who belongs to the same age as another one is his. — **Contemporary**

650. Person who does not feel gratefulness for other's help in times of need. — **Ingrate**

651. Person who believes in enjoying life and indulges in good food and other enjoyments of life. — **Epicure**

652. Person who helps a criminal in committing crime is his.— **Accomplice**

653. Person who lives on alms received by begging. — **Mendicant**

654. Person who belives that everything depends on luck. — **Fatalist**

655. Person who assumes false identity of someone else in order to deceive others. — **Impostor**

656. Person of supernatural powers who is considered as agent of god for spreading god's message to people. — **Prophet**

657. Person of supernatural power who reveals occult phenomena to the people. — **Oracle**

658. Person who dies without demising his properties through a will. — **Intestate**

659. Person who does not appreciate someone's good work is. — **Inappreciative (person)**

660. Person who can't be met by someone needing his help. — **Inapproachable by someone**

661. Person who is a voracious eater is a. — **Glutton**

662. Person who writes inscriptions on a monument's walls (murals) in beautiful and decorative letters, or manuscripts of high aesthetic values. — **Calligrapher**

663. Person who is a police informer. — **Nark**

664. Person who talks arrogantly/an annoying child. — **Brat**

665. Person whose honesty, integrity can be easily purchased by bribe is a. — **Venal person**

666. Person who sells his services for earning money is a. — **Mercenary**

667. Piece of wood or paper used for kindling a fire. — **Spill/Fidibus**

668. Place where grains are stored. — **Granary**

669. Place where horses are kept. — **Stable**

670. Place (a large cage) where birds are kept. — **Aviary**

671. Place where wild animals are kept in their natural environs. — **Sanctuary**

672. Place where coins are legally fabricated or invented out of metals (non-ferrous metals). — **Mint**

673. Place where goods are stored. — **Depot**

674. Place where food articles are stored. — **Pantry**

675. Place where animals' hides are processed for making leather.— **Tannery**

676. Place where wine is produced. — **Brewery**

677. Place where soldiers are housed. — **Cantonment**

678. Place where soldiers are kept in civilian area with authorisation.— **Billet**

679. Place where milk and milk products are produced. — **Dairy**

680. Place where aeroplanes are kept when not in use. — **Hangar**

681. Place where people do physical exercises for fitness. — **Gymnasium**

682. Place where orphan children are kept and looked after.— **Orphanage**

683. Place where tourists go for enjoyment. — **Resort**

684. Place where antiques are kept. — **Museum**

685. Place where valuable papers, files, articles are kept stored for future use. — **Archive**

686. Place where travellers take rest. — **Inn**

687. Place which is difficult to reach to is. — **Inaccessible place**

688. Place of study or training in a particular field of knowledge is. — **Academy**

689. Plant which belongs to a place since the earliest times; or pertaining to ideas unrelated to a person's train of thoughts which come into the mind. — **Autochthon**

690. Place where someone can live or stay is. — **Accommodation**

691. Place where important documents are kept for perservation is. — **Archive**

692. Place under control of an emperor. — **Empire**

693. Place under control of the Nature of creator of the world. — **Realm**

694. Place under control of a legal authority. — **Jurisdiction**

695. Place under one's command. — **Domain**

696. Place where a saint lives in solitude for religious purposes.— **Hermitage**

697. Place where large number of people stay by sharing a large room. — **Dormitory**

698. Place in a town where people of minority community inhabit, e.g. Jews quarters in Italian or other atics where they are confined. — **Ghetto**

699. Place where ill persons or needy, homeless ones are accommodated as charity. — **Hospice**

700. Place where people assemble to meet at appointed time. — **Rendezvous**

701. Place of stay made of ice blocks where Eskimos live. — **Igloo**

702. Place of stay where priests and nuns live. — **Monastery**

703. Place where pigs are kept. — **Stye**

704. Place where dogs are kept. — **Kennel**

705. Place where lions live or are kept. — **Den/Lair**

706. Place where farm animals are kept. — **Pen**

707. Place behind kitchen where dirty kitchenware is washed. — **Scullery**

708. Place in desert where water is available. — **Oasis**

709. Place where secret meeting is held by thieves, robbers, spy agents, etc. — **Assignation**

710. Place where lovers meet secretly. — **Tryst**

711. Place where people assemble at a pre-fixed timing by coming from different areas, usually for gossipping. — **Rendezvous**

712. Place where wild animals are kept for exhibiting. — **Menagerie**

713. Place where dead bodies are kept before being taken away for cremation. — **Mortuary**

714. Place where deadbodies are cremated. — **Crematorium**

715. Platform, usually made of bamboo, which is used to keep a deadbody on. — **Bier**

716. Platform on which a clergy in church stands to deliver sermon or raised structure for preachers to preach or the auctioneer's desk. — **Pulpit**

717. Platform on which religious offerings/sacrifices are made. — **Altar**

718. Platform on which public leaders stand to address electorates in elections; or election proceedings take place. — **Hustings**

719. Platform, usually decorated with flowers, on which deadbody lies in state. — **Catafalque**

720. Person who helps someone in committing an act of crime is his. — **Accomplice**

721. Person who is expert in an activity is an. — **Ace**

722. Person who performs gymnastic feats on a tight rope or erect pole, a rope dancer; a person who makes sudden changes or reversals in his opinions, relationships. — **Acrobat**

723. Person who is uncontrollably habituated to something injurious is an. — **Addict**

724. Person who remains faithful to his party or religion is an. — **Adherent**

725. Person who travels in space aboard a spacecraft is an. — **Aeronaut**

726. Person who appreciates the beauty of art is. — **Aesthete**

727. Person who is fond of a specific sporting activity or past time, such as bull-fighting, cricket, cinema etc. — **Aficionado**

728. Person who is related to someone by being descendant from the same male ancestor is. — **Agnate**

729. Person who is ignorant of the fact whether God exists or not is an. — **Agnostic**

730. Person who is believer of the existence of God is. — **Theist**

731. Person who is disbeliever of the existence of God is. — **Atheist**

732. Person who is an assistant to a public leader is. — **Aide**

733. Peson who is an assistant to a senior officer is. — **Subordinate**

734. Person who is an assistant to a criminal is. — **Henchman**

735. Person having white skin and hairs and pink eyes due to lack of skin pigment is an. — **Albino**

736. Person who belongs to other country/place than where he is living is an. — **Alien**

737. Person who is about to achieve adulthood. — **Adolescent**

738. Person who is opposed to someone is his. — **Adversary/Antagonist**

739. Person who insinuates into mob to provoke them to resort to violence. — **Agent provocateur**

740. Person who gives alms in charity. — **Almoner**

741. Person who belongs to noble section of society by birth.— **Aristocrat**

742. Person who wilfully indulges in setting public property on fire in violence. — **Arsonist**

743. Person who indulges in wilful looting or destroying of public property in mob violence. — **Vandal**

744. Person who moves from place to place to entertain people by composing and reciting epic or traditional folklores. — **Bard**

745. Person who rules with absolute authoritarian powers. — **Autocrat**

746. Person who rules with cruelty on people. — **Despot/Tyrant**

747. Person who is ill-reputed to indulge in promiscuous amorous relationships with serveral women. — **Casanova, Don Juan**

748. Person who is inspired with lofty but impractical ideas/ideals. — **Don Quixote**

749. Person who introduces a stage show to the audience before actors' performance so as to explain the theme or to laud the talented actors presented in the stage show. — **Compere**

750. Person who acts as an agent of a foreign business. — **Comprador**

751. Person who types text for publishing. — **Compositor**

752. Person who officially holds investigation into the cause of death of a person in doubtful circumstances. — **Coroner**

753. Person who is broad-minded and not prejudiced to provincialism in attitude. — **Cosmopolite/Cosmopolitan**

754. Person who is obsequiously servile to someone in power is his. — **Courtier**

755. Person who is in charge of taking care of antiques, animals in zoo, etc. — **Curator**

756. Person who exploits people's sentiments, passions, or emotions to win their following. — **Demagogue**

757. Person who advocates peaceful solution to problems with another country. — **Dove**

758. Person who advocates war as a solution to nation's problems with another country. — **Hawk**

759. Person who does menial, dull, hard work routinely. — **Drudge**

760. Person who indulges in odd patterns of behaviour. — **Eccentric**

761. Person who is wont to behave unpredictably. — **Freak**

762. Person who sells small wares like button, needles, ribbons, and other dress materials. — **Haberdasher**

763. Person who sells his professional skill as a writer, journalist, etc. by writing in someone's favour. — **Hack**

764. Person who exhibits characters of both the sexes. — **Hermaphrodite, Epicene**

765. Person who exhibits feminine character which is unmanly. — **Effeminate**

766. Person who is partly male and partly female having the toughness of a man and softness of a female. — **Androgyne**

767. Person who attacks cherished beliefs, or traditional and established values by denouncing as being superstitious. — **Iconoclastic**

768. Person who is so popular as to symbolise the society he belongs to. — **Icon**

769. Person who receives and entertains invited guests. — **Host**

770. Person who is ignorant. — **Ignoramus**

771. Person who lacks professional knowledge of a given subject as opposed to experts in that field. — **Laity/layman**

772. Person who practises idol worship. — **Idolator**

773. Person who deceives by assuming the character or identity or name of someone else. — **Impostor**

774. Person who organizes public entertainment programmes. — **Impresario**

775. Person who rises in revolt against lawful government and engages in armed struggle. — **Insurgent**

776. Person who is adept in wits, jokes and pranks which is entertaining to people. — **Jester**

777. Person who does not have any principle and is having base nature. — **Knave, Scoundrel**

778. Person who is playfully mischievous. — **Rogue, Rascal**

779. Person who is habitually lazy and so lags behind others in any activity. — **Laggard**

780. Person who works as a substitute for someone during his absence as his assistant; a temporary substitute for a doctor or a clergy. — **Locum tenens**

781. Person who holds the view that a ruler must act beyond the principle of morality in order to stay in power; political expediency is placed above morality. — **Machiavelli**

782. Person who is symbol of greed for money. — **Mammon**

783. Person who lives on begging as some sect's saints practise. — **Mendicant**

784. Person who does something for others, viz., a soldier who fights for foreign country against its enemy for money. — **Mercenary**

785. Person who is self-willed, does what he thinks right, and is not guided by anyone else. — **Maverick**

786. Person whose body size is extremely below normal. — **Midget, Pygmy, Dwarf**

787. Person who abnormally hates mankind in general. — **Misanthrope**

788. Person who abnormally hates womenfolk in general. — **Misogynist**

789. Person who indulges in creating public disorder. — **Miscreant**

790. Person who is habitually stupid. — **Moron**

791. Person who is habitually ill-tempered, gloomy. — **Morose**

792. Person who is habitually enarmoured with his own looks. — **Narcissus**

793. Person who is all powerful. — **Omnipotent**

794. Person who knows everything. — **Omniscient**

795. Person who adheres to traditional beliefs and conventions. — **Orthodox**

796. Person who is discarded by his own caste men, society. — **Outcast**

797. Person who is treated as untouchable by society. — **Pariah**

798. Person of ordinary class who becomes a rich person, influential or powerful without concomittant sophistication. — **Parvenu, Neorich, Upstart**

799. Person who holds honorary position in a set-up, or who supports a venture, organization as a distinguished person. — **Patron**

800. Person who takes to walk on road or pavement while going from a place to another place. — **Pedestrian**

801. Person who is welcome in company by others. — **Persona grata**

802. Person who is not welcome by others. — **Persona non grata**

803. Person who belongs to a group of robbers engaged in looting ships on high sea. — **Pirate**

804. Person in authority who is invested with full powers of acting or taking actions as he deems fit. — **Plenipotentiary**

805. Person who is sent to damnation by God for the sins committed by him. — **Reprobate**

806. Person who advocates radical change in a rotten system. — **Revolutionary**

807. Person who fights for protecting his religion from infidels.— **Crusader**

808. Person who indulges in unlawful activities, e.g., murder, robbery, playing pander for another. — **Ruffian**

809. Person who indulges in underhand damaging activities in one's own camp or by stealthily entering another camp. — **Saboteur**

810. Person who takes pleasure in inflicting pain on others. — **Sadist**

811. Person who takes pleasure in misery of others. — **Schadenfreude**

812. Person, creature or thing, whose presence assures good luck.— **Mascot**

813. Person who lives a life devoid of luxury on his own volition.— **Spartan**

814. Person who practises his profession as a lawyer by indulging in unfair means. — **Shyster**

815. Person who earns salary without doing commensurate job.— **Sinecurist**

816. Person who shows deep antipathy to foreigners or to foreign things. — **Xenophobe**

817. Person who is habitually dirty. — **Sloven**

818. Person who is well-known in social circle, and takes part in social gatherings. — **Socialite**

819. Person who is handicap with inability to control movements of limbs due to cerebral palsy. — **Spastic**

820. Person who takes possession of public land and starts living there due to having no place of his own to live in. — **Squatter**

821. Person who works as an agent for selling property, rail or games ticket for monetary gains. — **Tout**

822. Person who sells goods which are banned. — **Trafficker**

823. Person who lends money on premium rates of interest. — **Usurer**

824. Person who portrays bad character roles in cinema. — **Villain**

825. Person who has imaginative thinking and capacity to plan for the future. — **Visionary**

826. Person who enjoys gratification by looking at amorous activities or others, or by peeping into other's private affairs. — **Voyeur**

827. Person who is a vagabond. — **Waif**

828. Person who is adept in making facetious jokes. — **Wag**

829. Person who is a skilled fighter and takes part in war. —**Warrior**

830. Person who pretends to have great wisdom. — **Wiseacre**

831. Past student/students (male) of a college, school, or university is its. — **Alumnus/Alumni**

832. Past student/students (female) of a college, school, etc. is its. — **Alumna/Alumnae**

833. Person's close friend who is very much like him in his ego. — **Alter Ego**

834. Person who is concerned with the well-being of others instead of oneself is. — **Altruist**

835. Person who is a new entrant to a party or religion. — **Neophyte**

836. Person who is beginner in learning an art or work is. — **Callow**

837. Person who is a new hand in doing a job is. — **Novice/Tyro**

838. Person who is not expert in a field of art or music is. — **Amateur**

839. Person who is yet inexperienced in his job. — **Greenhorn**

840. Person who uses both his hands with equal ease in doing something is. — **Ambidextrous**

841. Person who is friendly in manners is. — **Amiable**

842. Person's earlier social background which is used to judge his character is his. — **Antecedent**

843. Phobia of height. — **Acrophobia**

844. Phobia of being present in open or public place. — **Agoraphobia**

845. Phobia of being present in a congested place. — **Claustrophobia**

846. Pot in which scented glues, agarbatti (incense) is burnt. — **Censer**

847. Pot in which flowers are kept in a room. — **Vase**

848. Politician who seeks to get elected from a constituency away from his home-place is. — **Carpetbagger**

849. Practice of marrying one's deceased brother's widow. — **Levirate**

850. Prayer for the repose of the soul of dead person. — **Requiem**

851. Prayer to God to save from crisis. — **Hosannah**

852. Prayer to be chanted in morning hours. — **Matins**

853. Prayer to be chanted in evening hours. — **Vespers**

854. Process of development of an organism by going through various stages of life. — **Evolution**

Words beginning with —— R ——

855. Rebirth of a dead one in new living human form. — **Reincarnation**

856. Recover health gradually after illness. — **Convalesce**

857. Remove a mistake or defect. — **Rectify**

858. Remove the cause of grievance. — **Redress**

859. Remove objectionable portion from a written text. — **Expunge**

860. Remove wrong notions about something from one's mind.— **Disabuse**

861. Rubbing of oil for purifying or consecrating someone is.— **Anointment**

862. Range of one's knowledge or understanding. — **Ken**

863. Remembering one's happy moments of past life. — **Reminiscence**

864. Remembering old days with sentimental longing for. — **Nostalgia**

865. Remaining/left-over portion of a felled tree. — **Stump**

866. Remaining portion of an used-up thing, such as pencil, cigarette, candle etc. — **Stub**

867. Reason of someone or something being in existence in this world. — **Raison d' etre**

868. Revival of old art, culture, fashion once again. — **Renaissance**

869. Recruitment of able-bodied persons compulsorily in army for defending the country. — **Conscription**

870. Rigidity of body occurring after the death. — **Rigor mortis**

Words beginning with — S —

871. Search for underground source of water by occult method of poking stick on the ground. — **Dowse**

872. Search for missing thing by turning around things all over a place. — **Rummage**

873. Search for usable materials in a heap or garbage. — **Scavenge**

874. Search for something in dark by moving hands all around to feel for it. — **Grope**

875. Search someone's body and pockets for objectionable things kept concealed. — **Frisk**

876. Shallow bed of a river through which we can cross it on feet. — **Ford**

877. Silent expression of one's emotions through body movement and facial expression. — **Pantomime**

878. Singer, usually a folk singer, who moves from village to village to entertain people. — **Minstrel**

879. Singer who tours villages to entertain people with songs on epics. — **Bard**

880. Skin which has become hard and insensitive due to constant friction or pressure on it. — **Callus**

881. Skin of dead animal which is removed to make leather. — **Hide**

882. Skin of animal with fur grown on it. — **Pelt**

883. Skin layer formed over a wound which finally falls down after wound is healed. — **Scurf**

884. Skin surrounding the edges of nails. — **Cuticle**

885. Story in which hidden message needs to be interpreted to reveal it is. **— Allegory**

886. Story which has no definite source as to who had said it is. **— Apocryphal story**

887. Substance that causes allergic reaction in one's body is. **— Allergen**

888. Someone who becomes centre of attention of all those present there is. **— Cynosure of all eyes**

889. Someone (or something) vehemently disliked by a person is his. **— Anathema**

890. Someone who is utterly hated by a person is his. **— Bete noire**

891. Someone who is untouchable for others in the society is a. **— Pariah**

892. Someone or something which suddenly appears like a ghost. **—Apparition**

893. Someone or something which represents direct opposite of something else is. **— Antithesis**

894. Something used to attract others so as to kill or trap is. **— Bait**

895. Something/someone used as a ploy to distract attention of someone else so as to deceive is. **— Decoy**

896. Something that is handed down by predecessor is. **— Legacy**

897. Something made from cross-breeding of two different species. **— Hybrid**

898. Something, viz., food, art etc., which does not suit the taste of common people and is appreciated only by those who are of refined taste and knowledge is called. **— Caviar to general or ordinary people**

899. Something which is passed on to successor. **— Legacy**

900. Something which is passed on to heir. **— Inheritance**

901. Something which is precious and so is preserved by people.**— Heritage**

902. Something produced magically by holy man in a gathering of devotees to impress upon them. **— Apport**

903. Song which is sung to mourn the death of someone. **— Dirge, Elegy**

904. Song which is sung in praise of someone. **— Encomium**

905. Song which is sung in praise of country, school, etc. **— Anthem**

906. Song which is sung in church by a group of singers (Choir). **— Carol**

907. Song which is sung by women on the occasion of marriage ceremony. **— Epithalamium**

908. Song which is sung to put a baby to sleep. — **Lullaby**

909. Sound of a heavy body falling on the ground. — **Thud**

910. Sound of horse's hoofs hitting the ground while running. — **Clop**

911. Sound of unoiled, loose joints of furniture, hinges etc. — **Creak**

912. Sound of sea waves hitting the shores and scattering of water.— **Splash**

913. Sound of forced walking through sticky mud produced upon taking legs out of mud. — **Squelch**

914. Sound produced by firing of machine gun. — **Staccato**

915. Sound produced by swift swinging of slender stick through the air. — **Swish**

916. Sound produed by releasing of stretched strings of musical instruments. — **Twang**

917. Sound produced by fast rotating wheels of a machine. — **Whir**

918. System of governance in which power is exercised by people. — **Democracy**

919. System of governance in which power is exercised by wealthy persons. — **Plutocracy**

920. System of governance in which rule is exercised by holy man. — **Theocracy**

921. System of governance in which power is exercised by officers. — **Bureaucracy**

922. System of governance in which a single person exercise power. — **Autocracy**

923. System which is under control of the government.— **Dirigible system**

924. System which is not under control of the government, and enjoys freedom of action decision etc. — **Laissez faire**

925. Shape of waxing or waning moon resembling a curved sickle. — **Crescent**

926. Shedding of old skin by a reptile, such as snake is. — **Ecdysis**

927. Shouting of crowd demanding once more of an artist's good performance. — **Encore**

928. Shouting of crowd to greet/acclaim someone. — **Hail**

929. Shouting of crowd wishing long life of a leader. — **Viva (long live!)**

930. Shouting of crowd expressing surprise. — **Wow**

931. Self-centered person is an. — **Egocentric**

932. Sardines, olives or any other wheat served before a meal or after soup. — **Hors d'oeuvre**

933. Subject over which one has complete knowledge. — **Province**

934. Successful venture or slogan which becomes popular and is joined by all and sundry. — **Bandwagon**

935. Stage during critical period in one's life when body functions, viz., fertility in women start declining. — **Climacteric**

936. Story which is in circulation through successive generations about a person, place, or heroic deeds. — **Legend**

Words beginning with —— T ——

937. Taking out working parts of a defunct machine so as to fit them in another similar machine requiring these parts. — **Cannibalise**

938. Teaching institution (school, college, or university) which one has passed from is his. — **Alma mater**

939. Terrifying experience in the past which keeps one haunting in present. — **Nightmare**

940. Tunnel or cave which is artificial and made in parks etc. — **Grotto**

941. Test of innocence through which a suspect is subjected. — **Ordeal**

942. Transmigration of a soul from the body of a dead person to another body, whether that of a human being or of an animal. — **Metempsyschosis**

943. Taking up a new life again in another form. — **Reincarnation**

944. Town's residential area, usually away from the market area.— **Uptown**

945. Town's market and business area – usually in the centre of the town. — **Downtown**

946. Time period in the long past – even before the great deluge which is supposed to have destroyed the world. — **Antediluvian**

947. Travelling by taking free lifts in passing vehicles en route. — **Hitch-hiking**

948. Travel planning and deciding on the routes to be taken in journey. — **Itinerary**

949. Tail or trunk of animal which can catch hold of something. — **Prehensile (tail or limb)**

Words beginning with —— U ——

950. Unfit to take part in contest due to injury or not fulfilling conditions stipulated (out of the competition). — **Hors concours**

951. Uprising of people against someone in authority due to injustice. — **Revolt**

952. Uprising of people against the government in order to overthrow it. — **Rebellion**

953. Uprising of troops against their own command. — **Mutiny**

954. Use of words in a sentence starting with same letter is.— **Alliteration**

955. Underground prison cell in a fort; the principal tower in a castle. — **Dungeon**

966. Unpredictable animal which causes damages without reason. — **Rogue animal**

957. Unpredictable weather which causes damages unexpectedly. — **Freak weather**

Words beginning with — W —

958. Walk arrogantly with stiff body as display of arrogance. — **Strut, Swagger**

959. Washing of hands and feet for religious performance. — **Ablution**

960. Waterfall which comes down in stages of rock surfaces. — **Cascade**

961. Waterfall which falls down headlong; a sheep cascade; an opaque condition of the lens of the eye — **Cataract**

962. Weak spot in an otherwise strong body is its. — **Achilles heel**

963. Word formed from combining from the initial letters or a group of letters of words in a set phrase. — **Acronym**

964. Woman having light complexion of skin and light colour of hairs is called a. — **Blonde**

965. Woman having dark-coloured hairs is called a. — **Brunette**

966. Woman whose husband lives away from home frequently or for prolonged periods; a woman who is separated, divorced or lives apart from her husband. — **Grass widow**

967. Woman warrior with tall and stout physique. — **Amazon**

968. Woman who is the head of the family. — **Matriarch**

969. Woman of dirty habits who is dressed shabbily. — **Slut**

970. Word or sentence which has been formed by re-arranging letters of another word or sentence is. — **Anagram**

971. Words written about the person on the tombstone over his grave. — **Epitaph**

972. Word which is unoffending and, therefore, substituted for a harsh, offending one. — **Euphemism**

973. Words related to a particular subject (e.g. legal term or medical term) which require special explanation listed in alphabetical order. — **Glossary**

974. Words with same spelling and pronunciation. — **Homonyms**

975. Words with same pronunciation but different spellings.— **Homophones**

976. Word which is the same when it is read backward. — **Palindrome**

977. Woman who is quarrelsome and bad tempered; a malignant man; a devil. — **Shrew**

978. What is sure to happen is. — **Inevitable**

979. What is likely to happen soon is. — **Imminent**

980. What is beyond doubt is. — **Indubitable**

981. What is directly opposite in nature or quality of something is its. — **Antithesis**

982. What is unfailing to be effective in delivering is. — **Infallible**

983. What is spotless. * Immaculate character. — **Immaculate**

984. What is so essential that it can't be avoided. — **Indispensable**

985. What can't be harmed. — **Invulnerable**

986. What can't be described in words. — **Ineffable**

987. Woman who is very attractive and seductive; one who leads man into difficult, dangerous or disastrous situations. — **Femme fatale**

988. Woman who lends her womb to another woman's foetus due to inability to deliver a child. — **Surrogate**

989. Woman who has round and plump body, and full bosomed.— **Buxom**

990. Woman who has manly courage. — **Virago**

991. Woman who attracts men, exploits & ruins them. — **Vampire**

992. Woman of loose morals or untidy. — **Trollop**

993. Woman of quarreling nature. — **Shrew**

994. Woman who is engaged to be married to a person is his. — **Fiancée**

995. Woman who sings and has very sweet melodious voice.— **Nightingale**

996. Woman who bewitches men to ruin them. — **Circe**

997. Woman oftenly aged one, who accompanies young woman or girl going out of home. — **Chaperone**

998. Woman who is a mistress of a gangster. — **Moll**

999. Woman who is very foxy in character; an ill-tempered or quarrelsome woman. —**Vixen**

1000. Woman who is habitually dirty in manners of living, dressing, etc. — **Slut/Slattern**

1001. Woman who remained unmarried. — **Spinster**

1002. Woman who is married but has not borne a child. — **Nullipara**

1003. Woman who has borne a child for the first time. — **Primipara**

1004. War which was fought between good and evil and was fierce and disastrous. — **Armageddon**

❑❑❑

TEST ON ONE WORD SUBSTITUTION

1. A country which comprises a number of islands instead of a large tract of territory is called ....
2. Habitual flatterer is called ....
3. Habitual servile to a person is his ....
4. Habitually suspicious to be suffering from imaginary ailments is a ....
5. Habitually over-concerned with one's health is a ....
6. A person who suffers from morbid fear of open, vast space, or market-place, and does not like to go there is said to suffer from ....
7. A person who is fearful of crowds is ....
8. A person who is fearful of closed space ....
9. A professional bull-fighter who earns by entertaining spectators with his fighting a ferocious bull is called a ....
10. A person who shows courtesy and considerate behaviour towards women in distress in public place and needs help, is a .... person.
11. A person who helps anyone in distress and needs help, is a ....
12. A person who substitutes himself or herself in place of another one in his or her role is his or her ....
13. A person who just failed to become what he wanted to be, say a doctor, is a ....
14. A person who deliberately pretends to be like someone, say an actor, by acting or adopting mannerisms, as he, too, wants to become like him is a ....
15. Process of development of a life or object coming into existence by going through various stages of changes is called ....
16. Process of a living organism undergoing change to different form is a ....
17. Woman of quarreling nature is called ....
18. A person with exceptional ability to hear from a distance which is not audible to common people is a ....
19. A delicate material which easily breaks down is called a .... material.

20. Our bones are hard and capable to bear impacts, but these, too, can break due to forceful impact, because our bones are ....
21. The policy of government control over business activities in the country is called ....
22. The policy of government's non-interference in business activities in the country is called ....
23. Something which is not fit for eating is ....
24. Something which is not fit for drinking is not ....
25. A land which is capable of producing sufficient crops is a .... land.
26. A woman who is capable to or has produced many children is a .... woman.
27. A woman who has grown old and is now incapable of bearing child is an ....
28. A writer who has written several books, and is capable of writing many more books is a .... writer.
29. A bomb which, when exploded, causes fire is called an .... bomb.
30. Time is a great healer – it makes one forget bereavement of one's most lovable person, because time is the most effective ....
31. A seductive and attractive woman who bewitches men is a ....
32. A woman who is habitually dirty in her living manners is called a ....
33. A man who is habitually dirty in his living manners is called a ....
34. A word with such spelling as to be the same when it is read from right to left, is called ....
35. An unoffending word which is used to substitute an offending word without change in meaning is called an .... for offending word.
36. Learning by cramming the lessons is called learning by ....
37. Crowd shouts .... in unison for demanding a performer or singer for more of his or her performance.
38. The patient's condition becoming worse again after improvement is called .... of the bad condition.
39. An inveterate criminal vows to shun crime after punishments, but he .... to the world of crime once again.

40. Bringing back the unity amongst people is to .... them.
41. Bringing back the lost or obsolete art or culture is called its ....
42. Style of writing in which author uses words in a sentence which start with the same letter is called ....
43. Fearful foreboding of unpleasant occurrence is called ....
44. A medicine which induces sleep is a .... medicine.
45. An unpredicted storm which suddenly hits a place is called a .... storm.
46. Born again as another living body is to ....
47. To return the loan and take back what was pledged in return is to .... it.
48. Underground prison cell in a fort of yore is ....
49. A regime which is dominated by rich people is called ....
50. A regime which is dominated by people belonging to uncultured, lower strata of society is called ....
51. Animal which has only one horn on its head is an ....
52. The process of moulting skin by a snake is called ....
53. An untouchable of the society is called ....
54. A person's most hated person is his ....
55. A shape of a sickle is called a .... shape.
56. Arranging in pairs is called ....
57. A man who eats flesh of humans is called a ....
58. Evening just before an important day is called .... of that day.
59. Hair on the back of an animal which is hard and erect is called ....
60. Main substance of accusation against someone is called the .... of charges.
61. Grinding of teeth during sleep is called ....
62. A period of time which seems to be endless is ....
63. Inspiration of doing something is called ....
64. Taking away rights to vote is called ....
65. Migration of the soul after death of a person into the body of another one born is called ....
66. A very close friend of yours in your ....

67. What is used to allure someone is called ....

68. What is used to distract attention is called ....

69. The person who has passed out of an institution is called its ....

70. The women who have passed out of a woman's college are called its ....

71. The institution / college from which you have received your education is your ....

72. Staying place of the nuns and priests is called ....

73. Staying place of a saint is called ....

74. The house of Eskimos is called ....

75. The washing room behind the kitchen where dishes are washed and cleaned is called ....

76. The person who is very fond of his wife is .... person.

77. The mother who is very fond of her kids is a .... mother.

78. The part of a town where minority community inhabits is called ....

79. The practice of marrying out of one's own community is called ....

80. Putting troops in a civilian area like schools, etc. when they are away from their base is to .... them in such a place.

81. Valuable objects which are preserved by successive generations in a family is called ....

82. Compulsory recruitment of young persons in army at the time of war is called ....

83. Matured child at an early age is a .... child.

84. An extraordinary skilled worker is a .... worker.

85. A person who likes to enjoy life is a ....

86. An artificial cave made in a place like park for entertainment purpose is a ....

87. Artistic objects made of clay are called ....

88. A lover of some kind of sport is .... of that sport.

89. The starter item in a feast which is taken as an appetizer is called ....

90. The most attractive item in a feast is called ....

91. Criminal who flees from one place to another in order to avoid arrest is a ....

92. One who habitually absents himself from the place where he is supposed to be, like a worker from his workplace, or a student from his school, is called a ....

93. Honour-killing of a girl by her brother is called ....

94. The soft covering of banana is called its ....

95. Sharp-edged pieces of a broken glass or an exploded bomb is called ....

96. The written work of an author which is published after the death of the author is called ....

97. An elderly woman who used to accompany a young girl going out of her home to market or in a social function and is supposed to keep watch on her is called ....

98. A young boy who accompanies an elderly lady while going out of house, and is supposed to be in her attendance is called ....

99. Sentimental longing of past happy days in one's life is called ....

100. The happiest period in one's life is called ....

101. A person who cleans utensils and dirty kitchenware is called.............

102. A person who is wise enough to see through the bad intention of someone in touch is a .... person.

103. A person of clean intention whose motive is easily known to others is a .... person.

104. The main area of a town where markets and offices are located is called ....

105. A story which carries hidden moral message which can be revealed by interpreting it is called ....

106. What can be perceived by being tough is ....

107. A limb of animal used to catch something is called .... limb.

108. A person without a fixed place of stay is a ....

109. One who is an expert in making maps is a ....

110. Growing fruits is called ....

111. The day of equal day and night is called an ....

112. Kid who has just started to learn walking on his feet is called a ....

113. Consecration of a deity by rubbing it with oil is called .... of the deity.

114. One who pretends to be a learned person is a ....

115. A piece of wood taken out of a log is ....

116. All the equal partners of a property are ....

117. The area of one's knowledge is his ....

118. The group of persons who are knowledgeable about a subject is ....

119. One who has doubting habit, and does not believe in something without covincing proof is a ....

120. One who is new in a job is a ....

121. The river-side area is called ....

122. Migration of people from their homes in a large number is called .... of people.

123. One who is not choosy in eating and takes whatever he gets is called .... person.

124. Spreading out of inhabitants of a place all over the world is called ....

125. One who is in a habit of impressing others by demonstrating his knowledge is a ....

126. Weeping of women on death of someone in the family is to ....

127. Medicine which is supposed to protect us from getting affected with a disease is a .... medicine.

128. Morbid fear of seeing a deadbody is ....

129. Small pieces of a broken ceramic ware is called ....

130. A person hired to clap in a gathering for someone is called a ....

131. The mourners who join a funeral procession are called ....

132. A number of symptoms appearing in a disease is called .... of the disease.

133. Hearing body sounds with the help of stethoscope or other medical instruments is called ....

134. Hairfall resulting in baldness is called ....

135. Inability to feel smell of things is called ....

136. Peculiar style of speaking to announce what a hawker is selling is called his ....

137. Inability to bear lights and hence liking to remain in dark place is called ....

138. Folding paper-sheet into various figures is an art called ....

139. Aversion to food caused by mania of losing body weight in order to maintain good figures is called ....

140. The campus of a building is called its ....

141. Inactivity in a living-being during the winter season is called ....

142. Travelling daily between home and office is called ....

143. A communicable disease which spreads by touching an infected person is called .... disease.

144. The system of keeping a patient infected with contagious disease aloof from others to check disease from spreading is called ....

145. An attempt to do something for the first time is called .... attempt.

146. Remains of the ruin of something damaged is called ....

147. Remains of the ruin of a demolished building is called ....

148. Broken pieces of stone is called ....

149. Inaugural show of a film is called its ....

150. No amount of entreaties and prayers can please the god of death because Yamraj is said to be ....

151. The strongest army is ....

152. The feeling that you have seen a ghost in the darkness is an ....

153. Mercy killing of someone in an unbearable condition is called ....

154. Medals and laurels which are hung on the uniform of a military officer are called ....

155. Something considered an object of irrational reverence is to make .... of it.

156. An item given by a person to you which you preserve as a memory of the person who gave it to you is called ....

157. An item preserved by you as a token of a place visited from where you had brought it is called ....

158. Uncontrolled physical urge for something is called one's .... to it.

159. Product which is produced locally is called .... product.

160. Free hand granted to someone to take a decision as he deems fit is to grant him ....

161. Narrow path through rows of chairs is called ....

162. Narrow passage passing through rows of buildings, or through a park, garden, etc. is called ....

163. Thickened skin on toes which is caused by constant friction of shoes is called ....

164. Crowd of fishes which swim together in the sea is called ....

165. Bees collect .... from flowers to turn it into honey.

166. A sudden feeling coming to one's mind without any apparent reason is called ....

167. A feeling coming to one's mind about something bad which is imminent to happen is called ....

168. A natural reaction in response to an external stimulus is called ....

169. What is not concerned with matters of morality is ....

170. Buildings, monuments, etc. which are important and needed to be preserved for posterity are called ....

171. A person who had held the office earlier to the present one is called the latter's ....

172. A new entrant to a party or religion is called ....

173. An unselfish person who puts others' interest above his own is called an ....

174. One who is adept in using his left hand is called ....

175. Information about a person's past activities which helps determine his character is called his ....

176. Important documents are safely kept in a place called ....

177. A patch of greenery which indicates the presence of water in a desert is called ....

178. The staying place of dogs, where dogs are kept is called ....

179. A natural successor to ancestral property is called ....

180. An event which is considered indicative of something important imminent arrival is called.................

181. A young and handsome person is called ....

182. A person who is very conscious of his good appearance, and, therefore, keeps himself dressed up is called ....

183. One who does not observe orthodox religious practices is called ....

184. A go-between who facilitates two negotiating parties reach an agreement is called ....

185. One who excessively boasts about himself is a ....

186. One wears a good look by dyeing one's .... hairs.

187. Lying inactive before eruption of a volcano is called it's lying ....

188. An opinion expressed in mutually contradictory language is an.................opinion.

189. One who has white skin and white hairs due to acute lack of melanin in his skin is called ....

190. One who has black hairs and black skin due to excessive melanin under skin is called ....

191. The killer of a public leader is called ....

192. One who leads a life which is very simple and devoid of even minimal luxury is called ....

193. An insidious cruel person is called ....

194. One who enjoys music even though he is not a connoisseur of it is called ....

195. One who commits unforgivable serious sin is called a ....

196. One who destroys his own creator is a ....

197. The sufferings undergone by someone in order to prove his innocence are called ....

198. The stickler of discipline is called a ....

199. One who does not drink wine is a ....

200. One who lives in caves is called ....

Choose the appropriate option out of the given ones which fits in the meaning of the word mentioned at the top of the options:

201. Slattern

(A) A woman who is habitually dirty and looks untidy.

(B) A man who is habitually dirty and looks shabby.

(C) A boy who has dirty manners.

(D) A person of loose morals.

202. Cognoscenti

(A) The people who are knowledgeable in a specified area of knowledge.

(B) The people who are able to recognize the problems faced by the society.

(C) A person who travels without being recognized in order to study the problems faced by general people.

(D) An expert who is knowledgeable in many areas of knowledge.

203. Nepenthes

(A) A medicine which helps people forget the unpleasant memories.

(B) A medicine which makes one forget death of a family member in due course of time.

(C) A wine which makes a drunkard forget worries.

(D) A drink which makes a drinker forget everything which he does not want to remember.

204. Charlatan

(A) A cheat who does not spare anyone from cheating.

(B) A person who advertises his knowledge and skill about a subject.

(C) A quack who pretends to have great knowledge.

(D) A fool who behaves as if he were a learned person.

205. Prodigious

(A) Extraordinary in talent before attaining the age of maturity.

(B) Having the tendency to behave as a monster.

(C) Having the tendency to waste money recklessly on unnecessary showmanship.

(D) (Something) regarded as extraordinary in importance.

206. Chaperon

(A) A person who flatters others for obtaining something.

(B) A servant who accompanies his master wherever he goes.

(C) An old woman who accompanies a young girl when she goes out to some place.

(D) A young boy who accompanies a woman wherever she goes out of her house.

207. Metamorphosis

(A) A process of undergoing change in some form.

(B) A situation is which someone undergoes degeneration into a bad shape.

(C) A change from unsatisfactory situation to that of an improved one.

(D) A situation in which any change in the condition of something is not possible.

208. Renaissance

(A) Revival of an art after vanishing in the past.

(B) Rebirth of dead person in another life.

(C) The soul of a dead person leaving the body to take another body of the person who has been just born

(D) The cycle of birth and death which occurs alternately.

209. Fugitive

(A) A boy who escapes from his school in order to avoid his classes.

(B) A boy who escapes from his house and loiters in mark and parks to pass time.

(C) A criminal who escapes from captivity and avoids being arrested.

(D) A criminal who surrenders to the court on his own volition.

210. Scullery

(A) A room where food is cooked in the running trains.

(B) A room where the dirty utensils are washed and cleaned for re-use.

(C) A person who washes the dirty utensils in a feast, and keeps the cleaned plates on the dining table.

(D) A hall where food is cooked and the dirty plates are cleaned.

211. Posthumous

(A) An author whose book is published after his death.

(B) A book which is published after its author's death.

(C) An author whose last book is published before his death.

(D) A book that is published before its author's death.

212. Effete

(A) (A woman) unable to bear a baby due to overage or weakness.

(B) (A woman) who has never borne a baby.

(C) (A woman) who has borne many babies.

(D) (A woman) capable of bearing a baby.

213. Crescent

(A) In the shape of a curved moon (in its first quarter).

(B) In the shape of a moon.

(C) In the shape of a curve.

(D) In the shape of a sickle.

214. Heirloom

(A) The prized possession of a family which is preserved by successive generations.

(B) The property obtained by a heir.

(C) Succession of heirs from generation to generation.

(D) A group of heirs who share the property of an ancestor.

215. Legacy

(A) Anything left by the predecessor to be handed over to the successor.

(B) The office of a legate.

(C) The property bequested by an ancestor.

(D) The legal office held by someone.

216. Valetudinarian

(A) A person who is very concerned about his bad health.

(B) A person who suffers from bad health.

(C) A person who suffers from imaginary health problems.

(D) A person who has become invalid due to ill health.

217. Archipelago

(A) An island country in the midst of a sea.

(B) A country comprising a number of islands.

(C) A group of islands in the midst of a sea.

(D) A large-sized island in a sea.

218. Prolific

(A) Capable of producing much or many, highly productive.

(B) Spreading in all the directions by growing.

(C) Rapidly spreading in all the directions by growing.

(D) Spreading in the forward direction.

219. Prolix

(A) Unnecessarily lengthy (speech or writing).

(B) Existing for a long time.

(C) Extended to a long period.

(D) Flowing forward like a liquid.

220. Martinet

(A) A strict person who does not tolerate indiscipline.

(B) A disciplined person.

(C) A person who oversees discipline in the armed forces.

(D) A person who does not like excessive discipline.

221. Fop

(A) Dandy. (B) Handsome person.

(C) Fashion lover. (D) Fail.

222. Frankenstein

(A) A person who is frank in dealings.

(B) A monster.

(C) A monster who destroys its own creator.

(D) An ungrateful person who deceives the very person who has helped.

223. Hearse

(A) A horse-driven carriage.

(B) A carriage to carry a deadbody to the burial ground.

(C) A carriage to carry the people from one place to another.

(D) A stand for holding candles which is kept in a room.

224. Cortège

(A) The people who attend a funeral of a dead person.

(B) The procession of the mourners accompanying a funeral procession.

(C) The decoration of a pandal for a celebration.

(D) A group of people who move together to go to a place.

225. Altruist

(A) A truthful person.

(B) A person who always speaks the truth.

(C) A person who truly thinks about the good for others instead for himself.

(D) A selfish person.

226. Samaritan

(A) A resident of a desert.

(B) A person who helps people in distress.

(C) A person who actively fights for a public cause.

(D) A resident of samaristan.

227. Teetotaler

(A) A person who drinks tea too much.

(B) A person who does not drink tea at all.

(C) A person who drinks all types of drinks.

(D) A person who does not take alcoholic drinks at all.

228. Heretic

(A) A person who does not believe in religion.

(B) A person who does not obey religious command.

(C) A person who does not follow religious rituals.

(D) A person who holds opinions contrary to the established religious doctrines.

229. Dastard

(A) A wicked person.

(B) A cruel person.

(C) A coward.

(D) A cruel but coward person who commits mean acts of cruelty causing harm to innocent persons.

230. Memorabilia

(A) The objects preserved because of their associations with memorable persons or events.

(B) Remembrance of important events.

(C) Something fit for keeping in memory.

(D) A momorable event or occurrence.

231. Herald

(A) A person who announces official information to people with beating of drums for attracting their attention.

(B) A messenger who announces the imminent disastrous event.

(C) A messenger who brings forth happy news to people.

(D) An event which indicates another event to happen soon.

232. Hibernation

(A) The state of inactivity during the winter season.

(B) The state of inactivity during the summer season.

(C) Laziness caused by acute hot climate.

(D) Staying indoors in the rainy days and enjoy leisure.

233. Diaspora

(A) Dispersal of people to different places in search of job.

(B) People of a country spreading throughout the world.

(C) People of a country who have spread in various parts of the world to settle there.

(D) People of a country who have been driven out of the country.

234. Anorexia

(A) Inability to eat due to nausea.

(B) Inability to eat due to upset stomach.

(C) Aversion from eating due to anxiety of putting on weight and get fatter and unattractive body figure.

(D) Inability to eat due to psychological aversion from eating.

235. Bulimia

(A) An abnormal desire for eating and feeling of constant hunger.

(B) Greediness of food.

(C) A habit of excessive eating.

(D) Abnormal feeling of hunger.

236. Ordeal

(A) Passing through torturous test, in order to prove innocence by an accused person

(B) Painful experience of punishment.

(C) Torturous punishment given to an accused.

(D) Order to punish an accused.

237. Oasis

(A) A patch of greenery in a desert.

(B) A matter of hope in an all-round atmosphere of gloom.

(C) An island in ocean with no easy access.

(D) A patch of fertile land surrounded by infertile land.

238. Heritage

(A) Historical places.

(B) Ancient monuments.

(C) Valuable structural wonders of the past which are considered worth preserving in their pristine form.

(D) Inherited property of ancestors by the heirs.

239. Dilettante

(A) An expert of specific form of art.

(B) A person who is not expert in, but merely enjoys, a specific form of art.

(C) A person who does not understand any form of art.

(D) A person who contributes money liberally to promote art.

240. Nectar

(A) A sweet drink.

(B) Honey produced by bees.

(C) The flower juice which is sucked by bees for making honey.

(D) An essence used to flavour drinks.

241. Premonition

(A) Intuition.

(B) A feeling of an event before it happens.

(C) A feeling of some bad occurrence which is imminent to happen soon.

(D) Feeling bad about something.

242. Ascetic

(A) A person who has become a saint.

(B) A person who lives a life like a saint.

(C) A person who lives a life devoid of luxury.

(D) A saint who lives on mountains.

243. Palindrome

(A) A race course for cycling competitions.

(B) A person who runs in the backward direction.

(C) A word which reads same when letters are reversed.

(D) A habit of running fast even if there is no urgency.

244. Ghetto

(A) A cave in a mountain.

(B) A ruined fort.

(C) The part of a town which is inhabitated by people of the minority community.

(D) The part of a village where the untouchables live.

245. Eternity

(A) A period of time with no beginning or end.

(B) An endless period.

(C) A very very long period.

(D) A life without death.

246. Precocious

(A) Maturing earlier than the normal time.

(B) Knowing before happening.

(C) Growing at a faster rate than usual.

(D) Having preconditions.

247. Sliver

(A) A piece of wood.

(B) A piece of torn cloth.

(C) A piece of broken glass.

(D) Splinter of wood, mental, glass etc.

248. Cartographer

(A) Photographer. (B) Chart maker.

(C) Map maker. (D) Photobin.

249. Redeem

(A) To buy back pledged materials.

(B) To restore.

(C) To retain.

(D) To fulfil a promise.

250. Grotto

(A) Artificial cave. (B) Tunnel.

(C) Castle. (D) Large cave.

251. Autochthon

(A) A native person. (B) Aborigine.

(C) Indigenous flora of a place.(D) Self-dependent.

252. Cant

(A) Chant prayer.

(B) Hawkers' peculiar manner of speaking.

(C) A speech which is not clear to others.

(D) Jargon.

253. Debris

(A) Scattered remains of a broken glass.

(B) Scattered remains of a vehicle involved in an accident.

(C) Scattered remains of a demolished building.

(D) Scattered garbage.

254. Fallacious

(A) Misleading. (B) False.

(C) Insincere. (D) Liable to fail.

255. Debutante

(A) An actor who acts in a film for the first time.

(B) An actress who acts for the first time in career.

(C) First-time screening of a new film.

(D) A person who takes part in a debate.

256. Proselyte

(A) A person who has parted with his religion and adopted another religion.

(B) A person who has deserted his party.

(C) A person who refuses to fulfil his promise.

(D) A person who changes his opinion for selfish gains.

257. Pioneer

(A) One who opens up a new area of knowledge.

(B) One who guides research.

(C) One who invents something.

(D) One who is expert in a field of knowledge.

258. Scion

(A) A young shoot of a plant.

(B) A young person of a notable family.

(C) A young bird.

(D) A young ruler.

259. Thrift

(A) To float on water.

(B) Miser.

(C) One who spends money carefully.

(D) One who spends money recklessly.

260. Mascot

(A) Symbol of good luck. (B) Puppet.

(C) Ghost. (D) Emblem.

261. Apocrypha

(A) Hidden secret. (B) Book written by unknown author.

(C) Cryptic remark. (D) Secret knowledge.

262. Paragon

(A) A model of excellence. (B) Rival.

(C) Unparalleled quality. (D) The most important person.

263. Toady

(A) Behaving like a toad. (B) Subservient.

(C) Sycophant. (D) Greedy person.

264. Matins

(A) Morning-time prayer. (B) Subservient.

(C) Sycophant. (D) Greedy person.

265. Matador

(A) Bull fighter.

(B) Gatekeeper in hotels.

(C) One who gives life defending the country from the enemy.

(D) A person who displays his adventurous skill.

266. Vagabond

(A) Vagrant. (B) Worthless person.

(C) Lazy person. (D) Touring.

267. Minstrel

(A) A singer.

(B) A folk singer who goes from village to village for singing.

(C) A folk singer.

(D) A drama actor.

268. Entrepreneur

(A) A person who starts a business.

(B) One who enters in a risky field of activity.

(C) A businessman.

(D) One who takes risk of doing something with uncertain outcome.

269. Quisling

(A) A traitor.

(B) Fifth columnist.

(C) One who sides with an enemy against his own country.

(D) One who sacrifices his life for his country.

270. Plutocracy

(A) The rule by experienced leaders.

(B) The rule by aristocrats.

(C) The rule by highly educated leaders.

(D) The rule by rich persons.

❑❑❑

ANSWERS

One Word Substitution

1. Archipelago
2. Sycophant
3. Toady
4. Hypochondriac
5. Valetudinarian
6. Agoraphobia
7. Ochlophobic
8. Claustrophobic
9. Matador
10. Chivalrous
11. Samaritan
12. Surrogate
13. Doctor manque
14. Wannabe
15. Evolution
16. Metamorphosis
17. Shrew
18. Clairsonant
19. Fragile
20. Frangible
21. Dirigible
22. Laissez-faire
23. Inedible
24. Potable
25. Fertile
26. Fecund
27. Effete
28. Prolific
29. Incendiary
30. Nepenthes
31. Femme fatale
32. Slut or slattern
33. Sloven
34. Palindrome
35. Euphemism
36. Rote
37. Encore
38. Relapse
39. Recidivate
40. Redintegrate them
41. Renaissance
42. Alliteration
43. Presentiment
44. Soporific
45. Freak
46. Re-incarnate
47. Redeem
48. Dungeon (mortgage or pledge)
49. Plutocracy
50. Plebeianism
51. Unicorn
52. Ecdysis
53. Pariah
54. Bete noire
55. Crescent
56. Gemination
57. Cannibal
58. Eve
59. Bristle
60. Gravamen
61. Bruxism
62. Eternity
63. Afflatus
64. Disenfranchise
65. Metempsycosis
66. Alter ego
67. Bait
68. Decoy
69. Alumnus
70. Alumnae
71. Alma mater
72. Monastery
73. Hermitage
74. Igloo
75. Scullery
76. Uxorious
77. Doting
78. Ghetto

79. Exogamy
80. Billet
81. Heirloom
82. Conscription
83. Precocious
84. Prodigious
85. Bon vivant
86. Grotto
87. Terracotta
88. Aficionado
89. Hors d'oeuvre
90. Piece d'resistance
91. Fugitive
92. Truant
93. Sororicide
94. Peel
95. Shrapnel
96. Posthumous
97. Chaperon
98. Gigolo
99. Nostalgia
100. Palmy days
101. Scullion
102. Perspicacious
103. Perspicuous
104. Downtown
105. Allegory
106. Tactile
107. Prehensile
108. Vagabond
109. Cartographer
110. Pomoculture
111. Equinox
112. Toddler
113. Anointing
114. Charlatan
115. Sliver
116. Coparceners
117. Ken
118. Cogniscenti
119. Sceptic or
120. Novice Skeptic
121. Riparian
122. Exodus
123. Omnivorous
124. Diaspora
125. Pedant
126. Keen
127. Prophylactic
128. Necrophobia
129. Shard
130. Claque
131. Cortege
132. Syndrome
133. Auscultation
134. Alopecia
135. Anosmia
136. Cant
137. Photophobia
138. Origami
139. Anorexia nervosa
140. Cynosure of Premises
141. Hibernation
142. Commuting
143. Contagious
144. Quarantine
145. Maiden
146. Debris
147. Rubble
148. Scree
149. Premiere
150. Inexorable
151. Invincible
152. Illusion
153. Euthanasia
154. Epaulettes
155. Fetish
156. Memorabilia
157. Souvenir
158. Addiction
159. Indigenous
160. Carte blanche
161. Aisle
162. Alley

163. Calus	164. Shoal
165. Nectar	166. Intuition
167. Premonition	168. Instinct
169. Unmoral	170. Heritage
171. Predecessor	172. Neophyte
173. Altruist	174. Sinistral
175. Antecedents	176. Archive
177. Oasis	178. Kennel
179. Heir	180. Herald
181. Adonis	182. Dandy/Fop
183. Heretic	184. Intermediary
185. Braggart	186. Grizzled
187. Dormant	188. Ambivalent
189. Albino	190. Brunette
191. Assassin	192. Ascetic
193. Dastard	194. Dilettante
195. Felon	196. Frankenstein
197. Ordeal	198. Martinet
199. Teetotaler	200. Troglodyte

201. (a)	202. (a)	203. (a)	204. (c)	205. (a)
206. (c)	207. (a)	208. (a)	209. (c)	210. (b)
211. (b)	212. (a)	213. (a)	214. (a)	215. (a)
216. (a)	217. (b)	218. (a)	219. (a)	220. (a)
221. (a)	222. (c)	223. (b)	224. (b)	225. (c)
226. (b)	227. (d)	228. (d)	229. (d)	230. (a)
231. (a)	232. (a)	233. (c)	234. (c)	235. (a)
236. (a)	237. (a)	238. (c)	239. (b)	240. (c)
241. (c)	242. (b)	243. (c)	244. (c)	245. (a)
246. (a)	247. (d)	248. (c)	249. (a)	250. (a)
251. (c)	252. (b)	253. (b)	254. (a)	255. (b)
256. (a)	257. (a)	258. (b)	259. (c)	260. (a)
261. (b)	262. (a)	263. (c)	264. (a)	265. (a)
266. (a)	267. (b)	268. (a)	269. (c)	270. (d)

❑❑❑

EXERCISE ON ONE WORD SUBSTITUTION

Give single word each which will appropriately subsititute each of the following :

1. One who takes pleasure in tormenting others.
2. One who feels pleasure to see someone in misery.
3. One who feels sexual pleasure in tormenting himself.
4. One who takes pleasure in prying into others' private affairs.
5. A companion of someone who behaves ridiculously to make his (some one's) behavior look more dignified.
6. An animal which feeds on whatever is available.
7. The sharp-edged pieces of broken material.
8. Simultaneous purchase and sale of the same securities, commodities or foreign exchange in different markets, with a view to profiteering from the differential in prices.
9. A book of an author which is published after his death.
10. Drawing similarity of two different things.
11. Drawing dis-similarity of two different things.
12. Never-ending period of time.
13. Evening prayer.
14. A female with dirty habits.
15. A male with dirty habits.
16. One who thinks about himself only.
17. One who thinks about others.
18. One who helps anyone who is in need of help.
19. Casting off of intugement by snakes.
20. Casting off of dead and dried leaves by trees in which place new leaves grow afresh.
21. A storm which suddenly builds up without any apparent cause.
22. Migration of the soul from a deadbody upon death to another living body.
23. Re-birth after death.
24. Old and obsolete form of art or culture becoming popular again.
25. Artificial leg which is fitted in place of amputated leg of a person.
26. The song which makes a baby sleep.
27. Public speech praising someone.
28. Educational institution of ex-students is their..........

29. A person who risks his life in fighting with men or animals in the arena for people's entertainment.
30. A person who starts his own business.
31. A person who is an influential businessman in a particular field of business.
32. An animal which eats meat of its own species.
33. An artist who makes various figures from a sheet of paper.
34. A person who makes stamp collection.
35. A tree which starts giving fruits earlier than usual time.
36. A baby who has just started to learn walking.
37. A disease which spreads by touch.
38. Snatching someone's voting rights.
39. Tricks used to deceive others.
40. Sense of self well-being which makes one feel satisfied.
41. Remains of a demolished house.
42. Doing something for the first time.
43. Grinding teeth in one's sleep.
44. River-side area of a place.
45. Medals and decorations displayed on a uniform.
46. Walking space passing through rows of seats in an auditorium.
47. Artefacts made of clay.
48. One who does not believe in something without proof.
49. One who claims to be a learned person.
50. A saint who lives in an isolated place to practise religious meditations.
51. What is vehemently hated by someone is his...........
52. A cow belongs to which animal species?
53. A grass-eating animal is called..................
54. Large boards which are used for advertising.
55. Social practice of marrying within one's own community.
56. Physical problems caused by medical treatments are called............
57. One who gets frightened on seeing a deadbody.
58. One who suffers from involuntary urination on the bed during sleep.
59. A man who accompanies an elderly woman.
60. Valuables which are kept preserved by successive generations of a family.
61. Using less harsh words to avoid unpleasantness associated with harsh words.
62. Writings on tombstone.

63. Prison cell made in the basement of a fort.
64. Tough time undergone to prove one's innocence.
65. A moral story to convey an useful lesson.
66. Hard skin caused by regular friction on the spot.
67. The most popular symbol of a particular field.
68. The youngest member of a prominent family.
69. The part of a town inhabited by the minority community.
70. Erect and hard hair which is used for making brush.

❑❑❑

ANSWERS

1. Sadist
2. Schadefreude
3. Sado masochist
4. Voyeur
5. Foil
6. Omnivorous
7. Shrapnel
8. Arbitrage
9. Posthumous
10. Analogy
11. Disparity
12. Eternity
13. Vespers
14. Slut
15. Sloven
16. Selfish
17. Altruist
18. Samaritan
19. Ecdysis
20. Shed
21. Freak storm
22. Metempsycosis
23. Re-incarnation
24. Renaissance
25. Prosthesis
26. Lullaby
27. Encomium
28. Alma mater
29. Gladiator
30. Entrepreneur
31. Tycoon
32. Cannibal
33. Origamist
34. Philatelist
35. Precocious tree
36. Toddler
37. Contagious disease
38. Dis-enfranchise
39. Artifice
40. Euphoria
41. Rubble
42. Maiden
43. Bruxism
44. Riparian
45. Epaulette
46. Aisle
47. Terracotta
48. Skeptic
49. Charlatan
50. Hermit
51. Bete noire
52. Bovine
53. Graminivorous
54. Hoarding
55. Endogamy
56. Iatrogenic problems
57. Necrophobist
58. Eneuresis
59. Gigolo
60. Heirloom
61. Euphemism
62. Epitaph
63. Dungeon
64. Ordeal
65. Allegory
66. Sclera
67. Icon
68. Scion
69. Ghetto
70. Bristle

❑❑❑